As You May Never See Us Again

The Civil War letters of George and Walter Battle 4th North Carolina Infantry

Coming of Age on the Front Lines of the War Between the States

1861 – 1865

Foreword by Joel Craig
Sharlene Baker

The
Scuppernong Press

Wake Forest, NC

As You May Never See Us Again:
The Civil War letters of George and Walter Battle
4th North Carolina Infantry
Coming of Age on the Front Lines of the War Between the States

Letters originally published as part of *Forget-me-Nots of the Civil War; A Romance, Containing Reminiscences and Original Letters of Two Confederate Soldiers*; Lauara Elizabeth Lee Battle; St. Louis, Missouri; A.R. Fleming Printing Co.; 1909.

Images used in this book were previously published in *Battles and Leaders of the Civil War*; Johnson, Robert U., and Clarence C. Buell, eds.; New York: The Century Company, 1887-88.

Second Printing

The Scuppernong Press
PO Box 1724
Wake Forest, NC 27588
www.scuppernongpress.com

Library of Congress Control Number: 2010929183

International Standard Book Number (ISBN) 978-0-9845529-0-0

Acknowledgments

Special thanks to J. Robert Boykin, III of Wilson, North Carolina, for helping us piece together the true identities of George and Walter Battle, the writers of these letters. While we knew they were the sons of a Wilson minister, we had no idea their father was one of the founders of Wake Forest College in 1834 (now Wake Forest University in Winston-Salem, North Carolina). Mr. Boykin's depth and breadth of knowledge about Wilson County is a gift to the county and to the state.

We would also like to thank the Wake Forest College Birthplace Society and College Museum in Wake Forest. At the eleventh hour, the museum let us check their records in order to verify that, indeed, the Reverend Amos J. Battle was one of the founders of Wake Forest College.

Editor's Note

In late fall of 1861, George Battle's commanding officer informed him that the Reverend Amos Johnston Battle, George's father, was requesting the teenager's discharge from the military. The well-known Reverend A. J. Battle, a prominent and influential minister at the time and one of the founders of Wake Forest College (now Wake Forest University), sought to have his son released because the boy had enlisted without permission.

This collection of war letters written by teenagers George and Walter Battle during their service in Company F, 4th North Carolina Regiment, CSA caught our eye in 2001 when Sharlene Baker found them in a quasi-fictional narrative called *Forget Me Nots of the Civil War: A Romance Containing Reminiscences and Original Letters of Two Confederate Soldiers*. We felt their daring and courageous story needed to be heard again. Underage, yet full of vitality and idealism, these boys were not just fighting for their country; they were fighting to protect their family's name.

Responding to his father's request, George writes in a letter dated November 2, 1861:

"I never was more surprised in my life, to hear that you had applied for my dismissal for, although I should like very much to go home, I do not like the idea of being discharged from the army on account of my age, for in size and strength I consider myself able to stand the campaign, and should I go home, I do not think that it would be entirely right for me to stay there when our coast is in such imminent peril. I compare this war to that of the revolutionary, when our ancestors fought for their liberty, that whoever remained neutral were considered Tories, and I think that when this war is over and peace is declared, those who had no hand in it will be considered in the same light as the Tories of old, and I have too much pride in me to allow others to gain the rights which I will possess, besides it would take two or three months before a discharge could be obtained. It took Mr. Bowden30 that long to get his son discharged. Captain Barnes is going to write and he will tell you all about it.

Published in 1909, the original book was written by Laura Elizabeth Lee Battle, a sister-in-law of George and Walter, who married their younger brother, Jesse Mercer Battle. Unfortunately for history's sake, Laura passed the boys off as her raucous stepbrothers rather than the highly educated boys of the Reverend A. J. Battle. This fiction created by Laura obscured the true lineage of the boys. No one can be sure why she concocted such a story; perhaps she thought having authentic Confederate letters written by real soldiers would increase the notoriety of the book. Whatever her reasons, history has now reclaimed these two brave souls and revealed their true identity.

According to Laura's own biography, she was born in Clayton in 1855 to a staunch abolitionist who couldn't make a living as a farmer because he refused to utilize slave labor. However, it is unclear whether the Reverend A.J. Battle, her father-in-law, was also an abolitionist. We do know that he was an avid supporter of Wake Forest College where he raised an astounding $21,000 for the school in 1838. Around 1853, some accounts have the Reverend A. J. Battle leaving the Baptist Church and joining the Disciples of Christ Church (otherwise known as the Christian Church), a denomination which hotly debated the merits of slavery at its General Convention in 1863.

Whether the Reverend Battle was an abolitionist like Laura's father or a neutralist as George intimates cannot be determined. Politics aside, the words of these teenage soldiers bring the war to life — unpretentious and undiluted — with an authenticity that is awe-inspiring.

Craig and Baker

Foreword

The American War Between the States was arguably the most traumatic period in our nation's history. The conflict divided not only the nation but local communities and even families. The state of North Carolina was no exception, while sympathizing with her fellow Southern states, North Carolina would be the next to last state to cast her lot with the Confederacy, seceding on May 20, 1861. In the small town of Wilson two brothers were about to be caught up in the whirlwind of war which was sweeping the nation.

Walter Raleigh Battle was born the day after Christmas, 1839, the son of a Baptist minister, Amos Johnston Battle, and his wife Margaret Hearne Parker Battle. Walter was the fifth child born to the couple, having been preceded by three sisters and one brother who had died in infancy. Four more children would follow, including George Boardman Battle who was born on February 22, 1845.

The election of Abraham Lincoln was quickly followed by the secession of the neighboring state of South Carolina. With the likelihood of coming hostilities, local residents formed militia companies and soon began drilling in the streets of the quiet town.

George and Walter Battle soon joined their friends and neighbors in the local company. George was just 16 years old, too young to enlist without consent; so the determined young man simply added two years to his age.

Within days of the bombardment of Fort Sumter near Charleston, SC, the governor of North Carolina ordered state troops to seize Fort Macon near Beaufort. On April 19, 1861, George and Walter, along with the rest of their company, arrived at Fort Macon where they received their first taste of military life. Here the boys occupied themselves by shooting at porpoises and collecting sea shells. Little did they realize what the next four years would bring.

From Fort Macon they traveled to Camp Hill, near Garysburg, NC, where they began drilling in earnest. On June 28, 1861, the men were formally mustered into service as Company F of the 4th North Carolina State Troops. Colonel George B. Anderson, a former West Pointer, was chosen to command the regiment. George Battle admiringly described the colonel as "a fine looking man, about six feet high, large and muscular, but not corpulent; a high, broad and intellectual forehead, bold face, and whiskers (shaped like Walter's), about a foot long." Apparently the Confederate authorities were also impressed with Anderson, for he was quickly placed in command of a brigade.

George and Walter first witnessed the realities of war upon reaching Manassas, VA, near the end of July. There, at the site of the war's first major battle, they viewed the blackened, half-buried corpses of the enemy which prompted young George to prophetically state "It made me shudder to think that perhaps I may be buried that way."

In the fall of 1861 George's father wrote to Captain Jesse Barnes, commander of Company F, requesting a discharge for his son due to his age. George, however, was of no mind to go home. He wrote his father pleading that he "was a minor in age, as you say, but I am a man in size and everything else, and fully able to be a soldier." George would remain with Company F.

The regiment spent the winter of 1861 at Manassas, the men daily growing more accustomed to the spartan life of a soldier. The two brothers fared well except for occasional bouts of homesickness. Walter gained a position as a clerk on the headquarters staff. In March of 1862, the regiment was ordered south with General Joseph E. Johnston to defend the capital of Richmond from the advancing Union army. During the cold, wet month of April they participated in the siege of Yorktown where Walter received a wound to his hand which sent him to a Richmond hospital.

By May of 1862 General George B. McClellan's Army of the Potomac had maneuvered to within seven miles of the Confederate capital. General Johnston concluded that he must attack McClellan's army before additional reinforcements, already advancing from the north, could reach him. On May 31st the attack came at a quiet crossroads known as Seven Pines. Confederate General D.H. Hill's division bore the brunt of the fighting, and among Hill's troops were the men of the 4th North Carolina.

The North Carolinians advanced through a swampy wood, wading through knee deep water until they reached a clearing where the Union forces awaited them. The Confederates had to cross 200 yards of open field in order to reach the Union breastworks, which were surrounded

Craig and Baker

by an abatis of felled trees. On their first attempt a hail of bullets and shells drove the men back to the cover of the woods. As reinforcements arrived, they once again charged across the muddy clearing. With men falling at every step, the Confederates surged over the works, driving the enemy before them.

The charge had been a costly one. Three color bearers were killed before Major Bryan Grimes grabbed the flag and carried it over the works. The regiment had lost 369 of the 678 men that had entered the battle. Twenty-three of the regiment's 29 officers lay dead or wounded. Captain Jesse Barnes was among the killed. Major Grimes proclaimed that "No braver men died that day than Captain Barnes." Among the mortally wounded was George Battle who had been shot in the head. George died on June 6th in a Richmond hospital at the tender age of 17. His death prompted his brother Walter to lament "I don't believe I will ever get over the death of George. The more I think of it, the more it affects me."

Another casualty of the battle at Seven Pines was General Johnston, the Confederate commander, who received a severe wound. The disabling of Johnston led to the appointment of General Robert E. Lee as commander of the army. Lee sent for reinforcements in the form of General Thomas "Stonewall" Jackson's army which had been operating in the Shenandoah Valley. With the arrival of Jackson, Lee prepared to counterattack the Union army and drive them from the Confederate capital. What followed was seven days of fierce fighting as the rejuvenated Confederates forced the cautious McClellan and his army to withdraw.

With McClellan's army temporarily immobilized, Lee turned to face a new threat in the form of General John Pope's Army of Virginia which was advancing towards Richmond from the north. While Hill's division protected Richmond, Lee and Pope clashed in the second battle on the plains of Manassas. The resulting Confederate victory forced the retreat of the Union forces back to Washington, DC.

The victory at Manassas opened the door for Lee to cross the Potomac and invade Maryland. General Hill's division would lead the way into enemy territory. Marching north with the army was Walter Battle.

On September 14th General Hill's division held Crampton's and

Fox's Gaps on strategic South Mountain against the Army of the Potomac as it advanced to crush Lee's divided forces. The 4th North Carolina played an important role in delaying the Union army while Lee consolidated his forces near the small community of Sharpsburg, Md.

On September 17th the armies clashed along the banks of Antietam Creek in what would become the bloodiest single day in American history. Once again Hill's division was in the thick of the fighting, holding a stretch of sunken farm road that would forever be known as "Bloody Lane." During the battle General Anderson was mortally wounded and it was Walter who helped dress the wound and carry the dying general "through a field that looked like it was impossible for a man to walk ten steps without being killed." General Hill noted in his report of the battle that "All the officers of this noble regiment present at Sharpsburg were killed or wounded." The 4th North Carolina marched away from Sharpsburg under the command of a sergeant.

Lee's army retreated across the Potomac and remained unmolested throughout the fall of 1862. In December, the Confederates again faced the Army of the Potomac under it's new commander, General Ambrose Burnside. Burnside battered his forces against the impregnable Confederate position overlooking the town of Fredricksburg, VA. The year of 1862 drew to a close with the two powerful armies still glowering at each other from opposite banks of the Rappahannock.

The spring of 1863 found yet another advance on Richmond by the Union army. This time the commander was General Joseph Hooker. Hooker stole a march on Lee and crossed the Rapidan above the Confederate left flank. With the Union army pressing him on both flanks, Lee was forced to take a desperate gamble. He divided his meager forces, sending General "Stonewall" Jackson and 26,000 troops on a flanking march through the tangled forests in the vicinity of Chancellorsville.

Jackson's attack caught the enemy by surprise and swept away Hooker's plans of bagging Lee and the Confederate army. As darkness fell, Jackson rode out to reconnoiter the Union position. It was at the moment of his greatest triumph that he was mistakenly fired upon by soldiers from a North Carolina regiment. The wounds would prove fatal both to Jackson and the Confederate cause.

On the following day, May 3rd, the Confederates resumed the at-

Craig and Baker

tack on the Union position. Once again the 4th North Carolina was in the thick of the fighting. At one point, after Virginia troops balked, the North Carolinians walked over top of their prone comrades in order to attack the enemy. The valiant North Carolinians pressed the attack with such ardor that they soon outdistanced their supporting troops and found themselves in danger of being surrounded. In the desperate fighting that followed the regiment suffered another 270 casualties, including every member of the color guard. General Stephen Ramseur complimented the regiment's colonel as "the gallant Grimes, of the Fourth North Carolina, whose conduct on other fields gave promise of what was fully realized on this."

The victory at Chancellorsville had been costly, but the loss of Jackson and the heavy casualties did not deter Lee from taking the offensive. In June of 1863 Lee's army once more crossed into northern territory. Walter, returning from home where he had been on furlough, rushed north to rejoin his regiment. Traveling through Maryland with a band of returning soldiers he arrived the day after the climatic Battle of Gettysburg only to find a defeated army retracing its steps back to Virginia.

During Walter's absence there had been considerable turnover amongst the headquarters staff. With many of his friends gone, Walter decided to return to the ranks of Company F. Here he would suffer the hardships and privations of the common soldier throughout the remainder of the war.

The spring of 1864 found General Ulysses S. Grant in charge of all the Union armies. Grant had come east to personally lead the advance against Lee and Richmond. Grant's campaign began in May and produced some of the bloodiest fighting of the war. Once again the armies returned to the heavily wooded region west of Fredricksburg, near the old Chancellorsville battlefield. Here the armies struggled in the confusing and bloody Battle of the Wilderness which left both sides battered and bruised. Grant pressed on however, and once again the two armies clashed near Spotsylvania Court House. Here in the early morning hours of May 12th a surprise attack by Union forces overran the Confederate defenses and threatened to destroy Lee's army.

Among the troops who rushed to fill the breach were the men of the 4th North Carolina. Along the muddy breastworks Walter witnessed fierce hand-to-hand fighting as men shot, clubbed and stabbed each other from opposite sides of the breastworks for 22 hours straight. Walter declared that it was "the hottest and hardest fought battle that has ever been on this continent." Even high ranking officers were forced to "lay as low in the trench and water as the men."

The two armies continued to spar with each other near Spotsylvania for another week. On May 19th a Confederate reconnaissance ran into Grant's rear guard near the Harris Farm and quickly found themselves hotly engaged. Walter received a minor flesh wound during the battle. Perhaps more serious than the wound was the exhaustion from which he had been suffering for several weeks. His weakened condition led to hospitalization in Richmond. From there he was sent home to recuperate, not returning to the regiment until the end of August.

Despite staggering casualties, Grant continued to drive relentlessly south towards the Confederate capitol. The Union advance finally ground to a halt before the strategic rail center at Petersburg, VA. Here the two armies faced each other until the last days of the war. Despite overwhelming odds, Lee knew that he must keep the strategic Shenandoah Valley open. To this end he dispatched General Jubal Early to drive out the Yankees and keep the vital supplies flowing. Early's initial success allowed him to cross the Potomac and threaten Washington. Grant responded by sending General Phil Sheridan and a small army to clear the valley of Confederates once and for all. Sheridan vowed to lay waste to the fertile valley to the extent that crows flying over it would "have to carry their provender with them."

On September 19th Sheridan struck the Confederates near the war-torn village of Winchester, VA. Despite stubborn opposition, Sheridan's forces routed the Confederates late in the day, capturing over 2,000 prisoners. Among those captured was Walter Battle who was taken to the Union prison at Point Lookout, MD. Walter wrote a short note from prison assuring the folks back home that he and his comrades were "in very good health." He remained in prison until November when he was exchanged and returned to the ranks.

As the final year of the war dawned, the Confederates in the trenches had begun to realize that the end was near. A candid Walter dejectedly wrote that "The greater part of the soldiers seem to be in low spirits and a good many say the Confederacy has gone up, and that we are whipped. I have never seen the men so discouraged before." Days later he added "If the men are not fed they will not stay with the army." It was during these dark days that Walter's younger brother Cullen had come of age to serve. Despite his wishes to have his brother close at hand, Walter pleaded with him to "take my advice and never join this Regiment." He had already lost one brother and scores of friends and neighbors.

At dawn on April 2, 1865, a massive Union attack breached the Confederate lines at Petersburg. The order to abandon Petersburg and Richmond was given. The final act of the four year drama had begun as Lee's army staggered west in a vain attempt to outrun Grant's victorious forces. On April 6th the Confederate rear guard was cut off and surrounded at Sailor's Creek, VA. Among the 6,000 Confederates captured that day was an exhausted and starving Walter Battle. Once again he found himself confined at Point Lookout, MD, where, unlike the rest of Lee's army who received paroles at Appomattox Court House, he remained until taking the Oath of Allegiance on June 23, 1865. Walter returned to war-torn North Carolina. Four years of hard campaigning had taken its toll on him. He died a few short years later on November 20, 1869, barely a month shy of his thirtieth birthday.

George and Walter Battle served in one of the hardest fought regiments in Robert E. Lee's Army of Northern Virginia. The 4th North Carolina had been in the hottest part of the fight on a dozen different battlefields. During its service the officers and men achieved a reputation second to none. General D. H. Hill referred to them as "This gallant regiment, which has never been surpassed by any troops in the world for gallantry, subordination, and propriety." General Bryan Grimes, who led the regiment in many of those bloody battles, wrote that the regiment "was not excelled in the Army of Northern Virginia and was noted for its *esprit de corps*."

The letters of George and Walter Battle are remarkable not because they record the bloody battles, the hardships of a soldier's life, or the loneliness of being far from home. They are remarkable because they echo the experiences of tens of thousands of southern boys who served the Confederacy during the dark and bloody years of 1861-1865.

As You May Never See Us Again

These letters document the life of the average Confederate soldier as he marched, fought and suffered through America's bloodiest war. Often the letters were written on scraps of wrapping paper or the backs of previously used stationary. Frequently they were written under trying circumstances, on the march, in line of battle, or even from a Union prison. Together they form a complete picture beginning in the heady spring days of 1861 as a euphoric South confidently predicts victory, and climaxing in disheartening spring of 1865 when a dying Confederacy breathes its last gasp.

Two young brothers had gone off to war as mere boys. Their experiences quickly hardened and molded them into veterans of the greatest army ever to march on American soil. One brother would die a hero's death while bravely charging the enemy; the other would carry on through unimaginable hardships; suffering wounds, disease and imprisonment until the physical and psychological toll would claim him in a subtler, but equally tragic way.

Joel Craig
Germantown, NY

As You May Never See Us Again

The Battle Brothers' Letters Home to North Carolina

George

Walter

FORT MACON[1], N. C., April 19, 1861

Dear Mother:[2]

Our company[3] arrived here this morning at 8 o'clock. We had to stay at Beaufort last night, the water being too rough to carry us over last night. I intended to have written last night while at Beaufort, but we were so completely worn out with hollowing, etc., that all of us got to bed as soon as possible, which was about 12 o'clock. We have been employed a little while this morning carrying barrels, etc. It was raining the whole time. They make no difference here for rain or anything else.

There is only about two or three hundred men here as yet. There are more men expected daily. Our company is the largest, the best looking (so said by the men here), that there is in the Fort.

George and Tom Stith[4] are down on the beach shooting porpoises. I had to borrow this piece of paper to write to you, George having the paper in his valise.

The company has this evening to look around. Tomorrow we have to commence drilling. George has just come in. He says he had lots of fun, and told me to tell you that he would write to you tomorrow. He found a good many curious looking shells, which he has put in his valise, to carry home. Blake asked me to say to Mr. Rhodes[5] that he was very well satisfied, indeed. The whole company is enjoying themselves very much. I will write to you again as soon as I hear from you. Please write to me often. Direct to Fort Macon, care of Capt. Jesse Barnes.

Your affectionate son, till death,

WALTER

FORT MACON, N. C., April 28, '61.

Dear Mother:

As there is a man going by Clayton tomorrow I thought I would write you a few lines, to let you know how we are getting along. We are enjoying ourselves as well as can be expected. We had prayers and singing this morning by Mr. Cobb.[6] He spoke of the injuries of the South in an eloquent manner.

For the last day or two we have been living on the victuals that the people sent down here. The first few days we had bread, butter, etc., but as they have given out we live on bread, fat meat and coffee. If Blake does not tell you, I wish you would please send Walter and me a cooked ham and some biscuits, with a few of those small round cakes, for the cakes that are sent down here for the company are usually taken care of by the officers and are hardly seen by the privates. Walter is upon his bunk enjoying himself finely and sends his love to you. I am going to try to get a furlough to go home before long, for I long to be home with you all. * * * I forgot to tell you that we did not have to drill or work either this Sunday like we did the last. You spoke of sending a mattress down to us, but you need not for we are getting along very well. We are ordered to stay down here three months without lief to go home in the meantime, so Col. Tew[7] says. Believe me as ever

Your loving son,
GEORGE

CAMP HILL,[8] N. C., July 9, 1861

Dear Mother:

We arrived here about night, the day we left Wilson, and having raised our tents prepared to get supper, which we got about 9 o'clock. We are encamped in an old pine field, which is very hot, but the other companies that were here before have a very pleasant oak grove on a hill. The Second regiment, under Col. Tew, are on the opposite side of the road. Our Col. Anderson[9] is a fine looking man, about six feet high, large and muscular, but not corpulent; a high, broad and intellectual forehead, bold face, and whiskers (shaped like Walter's), about a foot long.

It is different with us here to what it was in Fort Macon and Newbern, as we are now the same as regulars. We have to come under the general regulations of war. I do not think that we will leave here for some time yet, as the whole regiment has to be uniformed with state dress. We have not received anything, and have only drilled this morning. Capt. Hall[10], of the Irish Company of Wilmington, in Tew's regiment, had one of his men hung over a pole by the thumbs, but Col. Tew had him taken down. In Tew's regiment there are 200 men sick, and a great many have died already, but in ours there are only two in the hospital. Walter sends his love. When you write, direct Camp Hill, Company F., Fourth Regiment, infantry.

Goodbye.
Your affectionate son,
GEORGE

Dear Mother:

We arrived here yesterday, and had to walk about four miles to our camps, with our knapsacks on our backs, and everything necessary to soldiers. Before we left Camp Hill, we got our state uniform, blankets and all the accouterments. We were nearly worn out after having walked four miles to our encampment, the knapsack straps hurt our shoulders, besides the weight. We expect to leave here for Manassas to-day, but I do not think we will, as it is raining.

We are enjoying ourselves finely. I have not had anything to eat since yesterday morning, except some cake and apples. We slept on the ground last night, and I felt sorter chilly this morning, but we will soon get used to that. I must close now. Give my love to all.

Goodbye.
Your affectionate son,
GEORGE

Craig and Baker

My Dear Mother:

As George wrote two or three times since I have, I told him I would write when we got to Richmond. The first thing I knew this morning was that he was writing home, so I told him to leave some room for me and I would write some in his letter.

There is not much to write, as we are about four miles from the center of the city. We don't hear any news, though we heard yesterday that they were fighting at Manassas Gap[11] all day. We heard none of the particulars. Captain Rather expects to leave to-day, but I do not think we will. Col. Anderson came along with us. We left half of the regiment at Camp Hill (five companies). My opinion is that we will stay here until the other five companies come, and all of us leave together.

David Carter[12] and little lawyer Marsh[13] are both captains in our regiment. George got the bundle you sent him yesterday. We are enjoying camp life now to perfection. Heretofore we have had a plank floor, but now we pitch our tents, spread our blankets on the ground and sleep as sound as you please. I never slept better in my life than I did last night. If it stops raining this morning I expect to go up town shopping, and if I have time I want to have myself and George's likeness[14] taken together and send it home, as you may never see either of us again.

I can't tell you anything about Richmond yet, as we have not seen any part of it but one street, that was about four miles long, and led out of town to our camp. We are much obliged for the bed quilts.

They do us a great deal of good. We do not trouble ourselves to carry them, but roll them up in our tents. We got blankets before we left our camps. Some of them were the finest I ever saw. I was detailed to give the blankets and knapsacks out, so I kept the best out for all the boys in our tent. They are so fine and nice I hate to spread them on the ground.

Fitzgerald,[15] Henry Warren,[16] Billy Barnes,[17] Tom Stith, George and myself compose the inhabitants of our tent. We have a very respectable crowd. I like it much better than being in a room with the whole company. As we are we have just as nice and quiet a time of it as if we were in a private room.

Give my love to sisters, and believe me, as ever, your sincere and affectionate son,

WALTER.

P. S. I don't know where to tell you to direct your letters in future, as it is uncertain how long we stay here.

Craig and Baker

COMPANY F., FOURTH REGIMENT, N. C. STATE TROOPS.
NEAR MANASSAS JUNCTION, VA., July 31, 1861.

Dear Mother:

This is the first opportunity I have had of writing to you since I've been here. We do not live as well here as we have, but we make out very well. We have to walk about a mile for our water; as the ground is too rocky to dig a well we get it out of a spring. You can't imagine how much I wish to see you all, I long to be free to go where I please. But alas, there is no telling where I may be, for when we first came here we did not expect to stay here this long without having a fight.[18] I went over to the battle field last Sunday, and there met a most horrible sight, for it had been over a week after the fight, and the bodies of the men had been blackened by the burning sun and the horses had a most disagreeable smell.

On our going on the field the first object that met our gaze was a grave in which fifteen North Carolinans were buried. We next came to a Yankee who had only a little dust thrown over him. One of his hands was out, which looked very black, the skin peeling off, and you could see the inscission in it. The next which I noticed particularly had his face out and his white teeth looked horrible. The worms were eating the skin off his face. It made me shudder to think that perhaps I may be buried that way.

There are wounded prisoners all through the country in every house. I hope that peace will soon be declared, that we may enjoy the happiness with which we were once blest. I wish you all would write to me for I long to hear from you.

I suppose you heard about Frank T. running from the enemy; it is true, the officers told it. The General gave him his choice to have a Court Martial or be discharged through cowardice, and he took the latter.

We have our little bantams with us yet, and we intend that they shall crow in Washington City, which is only thirty-three miles off, if we live. I must close.

Goodbye,

Your affectionate son,

GEORGE.

Craig and Baker

MANASSAS JUNCTION, August 23, 1861.

My Dear Mother:

We received your letter this morning when John Clark[19] came. George wrote a day or two ago, which you had hardly received when you last wrote. There is no news of any kind worth writing. George and myself are both well at present. It has been raining here for nearly a week, and it is tolerably cool. This morning was very cool and chilly. It begins to feel like winter is fast approaching. You spoke of sending us some winter clothing. We would be very glad to have a good supply, as we shall suffer if not well clothed in this cold country. I can almost imagine now how cold it will be on top of these high hills when the winter winds come whistling around them. The following list of clothes will be as many as we shall need and can take care of conveniently. Two pairs of thick woolen shirts each, such as can be worn either next to the skin or over other shirts; two pairs of red flannel drawers each, and some woolen socks, that is everything that we shall need for the present. You can send them by express, and we shall get them. You need not attempt to come to see us, for it will be impossible for you to get here. Men are not even allowed to come after their sons to carry them home when they die with sickness in the service. I tell you this to save you the trouble and expense of coming so far and then having to go back without seeing us. It is a great deal harder to get back after you get here than it is to come.

Ed Harris is now here with us, he came day before yesterday. He will leave in the morning, and I shall send this letter by him. He got here through the influence of some members of Congress of his acquaintance in Richmond.

Give my love to all. Tell them to write often and let us hear all the news.

Good bye.
Your devoted son,

WALTER.

P. S. Please name my dog Nero and try to make him of some account. What is sister's address?[20]

Dear Mother:

As Walter has told you everything, I shall be at a loss what to say, but I cannot help writing when an opportunity presents itself. Our fare is bread and butter and occasionally a little honey. The two latter articles we buy. The nights have been rather cool of late, but we have not suffered any yet.

I wish some of you would write every day, for I do love to hear from home so much. I do not know what else to say, I only thought I would write to let you know that I was still in the land of the living. Write soon, some of you. Tell Dr. Harrell[21] that I shall endeavor to write to him soon. If you have an opportunity, I wish you would send some paper and envelopes, as every letter we send costs about ten cents, and that is too exorbitant a price. Give my love to all. Goodbye.

Your loving son,

GEORGE.

Dear Mother:

I would have written as soon as I received your letter if the box had come with it, but as the captain[22] could not bring them with him, he had to get them transported on freight, which did not arrive until yesterday. You never saw such a mess in your life, cakes molded, meat spoiled, etc. Everything was safe and sound in our box, which we rejoiced at very much, for we have not been faring the best for the last week or two. Tom Stith got a box which was full of cake and nearly every bit of it was spoiled.

I am thankful for the boots, which are a trifle too large but I reckon by the time that I put on two or three pairs of stockings, they will nearly fit me. We were all very glad to see the captain and we were also pleased to see the things he brought with him, which added so much to our comfort. Times are all very quiet about here. We hear firing on the Potomac nearly every day, though I heard some of the boys say that Mr. Christman[23] was collecting goods to bring to the soldiers. If such be the case I wish you would send me an old quilt or something as somebody has stolen my shawl and I think I shall need one this winter, but you need not send anything unless some one can bring it, for it will cost too much to get anything here. We are all well and if we had been sick our boxes would have cured us. Concerning what Jeff Davis[24] says, I don't think I shall take any notice of it at all, for there are already too many healthy young men skulking around home and I could not bear the disgrace of leaving the army because I was not eighteen years old, but shall stay in the service until the war is over. I must close now, give my love to all and tell them to write.

Goodbye.

Your loving son,

GEORGE.

MANASSAS JUNCTION, VA., October 24, 1861.

Dear Mother:

I received your letter this morning and was very glad to hear from you all, but was very sorry to hear that sister was sick. There were 544 prisoners brought in here yesterday morning from Leesburg,[25] an account of which you have seen in the paper ere now. They were sent off last night to Richmond. Blake and Jack Robinson[26] was detailed from our company to go as guard. Leesburg has since been taken by the enemy. Our forces retreated seven miles. The enemy are about to flank us and I think that we shall have to fight soon for I guess it is very galling to them to have so many of their men taken prisoners. We have had frost for several nights and it is already beginning to turn very cold, but we have not suffered any yet. I wear two pair of socks in my boots and they do very well, for it keeps the cold wind off my legs.

You were speaking of your hogs being fat. You ought to see these up here, they are so fat that they can hardly get along. The beeves that we have here are the fattest and prettiest I ever saw. They are generally large young cows, nearly twice as large as ours at home. I have often wished that you could have such at home. We have got thick overcoats from the government, with capes reaching below our elbows. They are of great service to us in standing guard. If we had a good dog and was allowed to shoot, we could live on rabbits, for I never saw so many in my life, the woods are full of them. If I only had Leo here now, I could get along very well. I don't want him to be an unruly dog, for he comes of such good breed that I would not like to hear of his being killed.

I should like to be at home in hog killing time, and wish I could see Tasso now, for I know he is a fine looking dog. I hope Walter's puppy will not turn out. I should like to be at home with you on Christmas, but the way affairs are going on now I do not think there is any likelihood of it, as for winter quarters, I do not expect that we will go into any at all, for the enemy pride themselves on standing the cold weather and I expect they will attack us in the dead of winter. We learned from the prisoners that the enemy intended to attack us in two or three days, but let them come when they will. I will insure them a very warm reception. Before this reaches you will have heard of L. Barnes'[27] death and also of Bowden's[28] discharge from the army on account of being a minor, etc. Lafayette's death has cast a deep gloom over the company, for he was a very much beloved member. I will be very glad to get those blankets but I would wait and send them by some one, as they might get lost by themselves. All send their love to you.

Give my love to all. Goodbye.

Your loving son,

GEORGE.

CAMP PICKINS, MANASSAS, VA., NOV. 2, 1861.

Dear Sir:

Yours of the 29th ult. was received to-day, contents duly noted, and I hasten to reply. I must confess to a feeling of surprise that you desire the discharge of your son, Mr. G. B. Lee, from service, as I was of the opinion that you had fully and determinedly given your consent to his serving in the army of the C. S. during the war. Yet, however much I should regret to see George leave us, as he has been with us so long and has been, though young, a strong, athletic and good soldier, you have my free consent to have him discharged. You will be the proper person to apply to the Government through the War Dept., for the same, where I doubt not, should you still desire him to leave, you can, by presenting the facts, after a while obtain his discharge. It is not in my power to do more than give my consent, which you now have. George expressed some surprise on receiving your letter, and says he don't want to leave. I, of course, do not deem it proper to give him any advice, but simply told him to write you whatever he might think proper, as of course you were the person to advise him, when you could. He has just handed me a letter to enclose to you with this. Whatever course you may pursue I shall willingly acquiesce in. If he is still left in my charge, I shall, as heretofore, advise and correct him and use every effort in my power to secure his happiness and welfare. Hoping to hear from you again and that my answer may be satisfactory, I remain,

Yours most respectfully,

J. S. BARNES.

Craig and Baker

MANASSAS JUNCTION, VA., November 2, 1861.

Dear Father:[29]

I received your letter this morning through Captain Barnes and I never was more surprised in my life, to hear that you had applied for my dismissal for, although I should like very much to go home, I do not like the idea of being discharged from the army on account of my age, for in size and strength I consider myself able to stand the campaign, and should I go home, I do not think that it would be entirely right for me to stay there when our coast is in such imminent peril. I compare this war to that of the revolutionary, when our ancestors fought for their liberty, that whoever remained neutral were considered Tories, and I think that when this war is over and peace is declared, those who had no hand in it will be considered in the same light as the Tories of old, and I have too much pride in me to allow others to gain the rights which I will possess, besides it would take two or three months before a discharge could be obtained. It took Mr. Bowden[30] that long to get his son discharged. Captain Barnes is going to write and he will tell you all about it.

I am very well satisfied here. I am treated well, and am permitted every indulgence which the army regulations will permit. All the boys wish me to stay. I am a minor in age, as you say, but I am a man in size and everything else, and fully able to be a soldier. Nothing would afford me greater pleasure than to be of service to you, but the Confederacy also needs my services. But if you still insist upon my coming home, you can write again. I expect Bowden pictured to you the darkest side of a soldier's life, but there is enough enjoyment blended with it to make a soldier's life very pleasant. I must close now, so goodbye,

Your loving son,

GEORGE.

MANASSAS JUNCTION, VA., December 9, 1861.

Dear Mother:

I received your letter some days since and was very glad to hear from you and would have answered immediately but Walter has gone to Richmond and I thought I would wait until he came back. He went with a detail of men to carry prisoners who were taken by the N. C. Cavalry. He came back day before yesterday and brought us several books to read. Among the prisoners was a deserter from the Federal camp. He was a Baron in Russia and being of an adventurous disposition, he came over to participate in a battle or two and accepted a Lieutenant's commission in the Federal army, but finding, as he said, that there was not a gentleman in the whole army, he deserted, took a horse and came into our camp and has been sent to Richmond for trial. Formerly he had a commission in the Russian army, which he showed to the people.

We are expecting a battle daily. Yesterday we were presented with a battle flag from General Beauregard,[31] consisting of white cloth crossed with blue. This is for us to fight under and also every other regiment has one. The enemy knows our national flag and had already tried to deceive us by hoisting it at their head. Now I guess we will deceive them next time.

Our company has been detached from the regiment for the purpose of taking charge of two batteries which another company has left. We are now relieved of a great deal of duty, for we only have to guard the batteries which take six men a day and that brings us on about once a week, and we drill occasionally. With that exception we have nothing to do, but if the regiment leaves to go into a fight our company goes also, and if the battle rages at this point we will give them a few grapes to eat and also a few shells to hide themselves in and then we will play ball with them for a while.

Walter is still at his old, or rather, new post, and has a great deal to do as the chief clerk is very sick. I hope we shall get a chance to come and see you before the winter is gone, but I have given up the idea of seeing you this Christmas, altogether, but after the fight I reckon we can get a chance to go home. Give my love to all and tell them to write soon.

Goodbye. I remain as ever,

Your loving son,

GEORGE.

MANASSAS JUNCTION, VA., January 16, 1862.

Dear Sister:[32]

I received your letter some days since and was very much rejoiced to hear from you, but I thought that you were a very long time in answering my last. It came at last and eagerly did I devour the contents and with what pleasure I lingered on every sentence, no tongue can tell. The description you gave of your tableau interested me very much, and I regret very much, not being able to have been there, as all such scenes always interest me so much, besides the desire of seeing you act. I think, myself, that you should have had your face painted, and that would have set off the piece a great deal. It is a pretty hard piece. Didn't you feel pretty scared? What does Dick act? Who was that sweetheart of yours that has been home four times? I should like to know him.

We have a hard time of it here now. The ground is covered with snow and then a sleet over that, and it is nearly as cold as the frozen regions, the winds come directly from mountains and blow around us like a regular hurricane. But we have now moved into our winter quarters, huge log hut, and we keep very comfortable, but it is nothing like home, home with its sweet recollections. As I sit and write I cannot refrain from gliding back into the past and enjoying the blessed memories of yore. But enough of indulging the imagination, for this is a sad reality and it will not do for my imagination to assume too large a sway. Tell Miss Myra that when I visit Washington I will call on her parents. I expect to go there soon, either as a visitor or captive, but I hope as the former. We will have a tableau before long, I expect, but I expect the scene will be played in a larger place than a hall. It will encompass several miles and will take several hours to perform it, but when it does come off it will end in a sad havoc. I am very thankful to you for those socks you knit for me, and when I wear them I shall think of you. All around me are asleep and the huge logs have sunk into large livid coals ever and anon emitting large

brilliant sparks, that cast a ghastly hue around the whole room, and I now think it time to close, so goodbye.

Your loving brother,

GEORGE.

MANASSAS JUNCTION, February 22, 1862.

Dear Mother:

I did not intend to write before the Captain came back, but as one of our men is going home on a sick furlough I though I would write a few lines to let you know how we are. I expect the Captain is at Richmond at the Inauguration of the President (Jeff Davis), if so he will be here by tomorrow night, and we are all anxiously waiting for his return, each one looking for a letter and a box of good things.

The weather is still very bad and there is an incessant rain since morning, the roads are so sloppy and rough that the wagons can hardly get along over them and very frequently we have our wood to carry on our shoulders to keep our fires burning, but nevertheless we are getting along nicely and not much incommoded from the inclemency of the weather.

To-day you will remember is my birthday, seventeen years old. In size I have been a man for sometime, and now I am nearly one in age. I do not feel as boyish as I did when I left home, for here we have to act the man whether we are or not, and it has been quite natural for me to do so. In the service is a splendid place to study human nature, you can very early find out what a man is. This war will be a benefit to me and an injury to others. Some seem to lose all pride for self, and like a brute are governed entirely by their animal passions. Such persons may be found kneeling at the shrine of Bacchus,[33] to such persons it is decidedly injurious. As for myself, I think it will be very beneficial, for I learn to take care of myself, think and act for myself. I now see how much education is needed, and I regret exceedingly not having applied myself more closely when I had the opportunity. If this war closes within the next year I intend to go to school again, and at the shrine of Minerva[34] seek that which I have never obtained.

20   *Craig and Baker*

One Company of the North Carolina Cavalry were taken prisoners the other day. I do not know which company. Was never in better health. Give love to all.

Your loving son,

GEORGE.

You must excuse such a disconnected letter for my mind is very much confused. Love to all, Miss Mollie[35] and everybody.

MANASSAS JUNCTION, VA., March 5, 1862.

Dear Mother:

As I have nothing to do to-day, I thought I would let you all know how we are getting along. The weather is still very bad, ground muddy and miry as it can be. We all have had orders to have our heavy baggage ready to send off at a moment's notice, and also to be ready for the field. The enemy is continually marching upon us, and I expect that we will be in a fight soon, but the enemy cannot do so much damage for they cannot bring their artillery along with them. I was vaccinated last week and my arm is now very sore. I am excused from duty on account of it. I wish you would please get a pair of bootlegs and have them footed for me, a thick double soled pair, that will stand anything, and well put up so that there will be no ripping, and send them by Pat Simms.[36] Ask him to take them along with him or Virgil,[37] and also send what they cost, for I don't reckon that you have the ready cash, and will send the money. Let the boots be No. 8, made so that they will fit him, for I guess our feet are pretty near the same size. If you cannot get a pair made, get a pair out of the store, for I am just almost out and there is none about here.

Tell my sisters I think they could answer my letters. I must close now. Give my love to all.

Your loving son,

GEORGE.

Don't get the boots if they cost exceeding $10.00.

RETREATING MANASSAS, March 14, 1862.

Dear Mother:

We are all well as can be expected from the situation that we are now in. We have retreated from Manassas on account of not being able to hold our position. We are now 25 miles from Manassas, across the Rappahannock, and camped upon a high hill that commands a splendid view of that part of the river, which the enemy is compelled to cross.

We left Manassas on Sunday night and traveled until about 1 o'clock. When we camped for the night, everything that we could not carry on our backs was burned up, and I can tell you that you cannot imagine how much we suffered on the march, which consisted of three days' traveling, loaded down with our baggage and equipment, sleeping on the hard, cold ground, feet sore, half fed on hard dry crackers and meat. Our lot was not to be envied, and it is amazing how we bore up under the circumstances. We have been at this place for a day or two, for what purpose I know not, unless it be for us to recruit up for another march. We have no tents here to sleep in, but we have made ourselves shelters out of cedar bushes. We all seem to flourish, nevertheless.

The night we left Manassas it was burnt down and I expect there was a million of goods consumed on that night, all the soldiers' clothes they could not carry with them and everything that could have been expected to be at such a place where everything was sent to this division of the army, all was burnt.

I do not know where to tell you to send your letters, for I do not know how long we will stay here, so I reckon you had better not write at all. When I get to a place where it is likely we will stay, I will write again at a better opportunity.

Give my love to all. Goodbye.

Your loving son,

GEORGE.

HDQTS. SPECIAL BRIGADE, NEAR RAPIDAN
STATION,[38] VA., March 23rd, 1862.

My Dear Mother:

We received your letter last night dated the 6th of March. 'Tis the first time any of us have heard from home within the last two weeks. We have had considerable excitement since you last heard from us. To-day, two weeks ago, we evacuated Manassas and have been moving to the rear ever since. We are now on the South side of the Rapidan River, where I think we will make a stand. But nothing is known for certain, I don't believe the Generals themselves know. The night we left Manassas (about sunset) we marched ten miles that night, stopped about two o'clock and slept on the ground with the sky for a covering. We haven't had a tent in two weeks. We are playing the soldier now in good earnest. The last three days we marched it rained every night just as soon as we would stop for the night. After walking all day, carrying your ALL on your back, then having to start a fire out doors without wood (we have no light wood) and cook your next day's ration, is pretty hard soldiering, I can assure you. Though the boys all seem to be cheerful. We have very little sickness and for the last ten days (a circumstance not known before since we have been in Virginia) we haven't had a man to die in the Regiment. Pat Simms and his recruits have not yet arrived, they were stopped at Gordonsville[39] some time ago, while we were making our retreat from Manassas. We expect them daily.

The Yankees have been some distance this side of Manassas. Our troupes had a little skirmish with them a day or two after we left, some of the Cavalry came in sight of our pickets. They fired on them and they disappeared, 'tis reported that they have gone back to Centerville,[40] perfectly non-plussed at our movement. The country we are now occupying is the prettiest and the most beautiful scenery you ever saw. We can see the mountains in the distance covered with snow, and when the sun shines it is sublime. We are on what is called the "Clark Mountain."[41] There is a mountain or rather hill, on a mountain, about a quarter of a mile off that commands a view of the country for miles around, some of the men are up there all the time. I intend to send this letter to Richmond to be mailed. I do not know that there is any communication between here and Richmond. We only got the old mail that was stopped at Gordonville. Mac Williams,[42] one of our company, is going to Richmond tomorrow on business. I will get him to mail it for me.

I do not see a word about this move in the papers, so I must think the Government is withholding it from them, to prevent the Yankees from obtaining information. Johnnie Dunham is still A. A. Genl.[43] of the Brigade and I am writing for him, though I do not have one third to do that I did at Manassas, as that was a regular military post. We had inspection to-day, to see how the guns, etc., were getting on after the hard usage and bad weather they have gone through lately.

Write soon. We may get all of your letters, though you might not get all of ours, unless mailed beyond Gordonsville. Give my love to all the family, Aunt and Claudia, etc. etc. I remain,

Your sincere and devoted son,

WALTER.

March 23rd, 1862.

Dear Mother:

As Walter did not mention me in his letter, I thought I would let you know that I am well. Walter has told you nearly everything that transpired on our tramp, so I have not anything to tell except the burning of the property at Manassas the same day that we left. We had been told to go to the Junction and get what things out of our boxes as we could carry on our backs, for the boxes would not be carried on the train. After we left, the town was set on fire, and I expect that a million dollars' worth of property

was consumed. We had to leave our little Bantam chickens, as we had no way to carry them. The first night of our march, I never suffered so much from fatigue in my life. When we did halt we fell on the ground and slept soundly until next morning. I do not expect you can hardly read this, as it is done by a log fire on my cartridge box. Must close. Good bye.

Your loving son,

GEORGE.

Craig and Baker

YORKTOWN, VA., April 13, 1862.

Dear Mother:

I commenced a letter to you the other day but was unable to finish it, being called off to participate in a slight skirmish with the Yankees. We arrived at this place last Thursday evening and having sent out our portion of the picket, of which I was one, we ate our hard bread and meat and laid on the hard, cold ground for the night, with the blankets we brought on our backs for a covering. On Friday we were ordered out, for the Yankees were about to attack us, our skirmishers went out towards the enemy for the purpose of drawing them within range of our batteries, the enemy came in sight with a long line of artillery and drew up in battle array about half a mile from our batteries, by that time there was some right hard fighting on the part of the skirmishers. About two o'clock p.m., our batteries opened upon them and they were returned with the greatest alacrity; bombs, shells and balls flew about promiscuously, but happily they did no damage on our side, nearly all of them going over our heads. We threw some shells that seemed to do damage with the Yankees, the way they scattered when the shell fell among them. One shell which came over us bursted and fell all around, one piece fell right between two of our boys, but no injury done. The firing continued until dark, in the time the skirmishers set fire to a large dwelling house, near the enemy's infantry and under the cover of the smoke they broke in on them and routed them, but they had soon to retreat for the Yanks turned their batteries upon them, after which hostilities ceased for the night. We lay in the entrenchments all night. Next morning, Saturday, the enemy was not to be seen. This morning we are expecting an attack again, and have been ordered into the entrenchments, but they have not made an attack yet.

Gen. Magruder[44] says that if they do not attack us to-day, that he will them to-morrow. We are exactly on the battle ground of

Washington and Cornwallis, but all that remains to be seen are the old breastworks of the British, which lie immediately behind ours. The Yankees hold the same position that Washington[45] did. There is also the place where Cornwallis surrendered his sword to Washington. Yorktown is the oldest place I ever saw. I do not believe that there is a single house that has been built in fifty years. As I was walking through the town, I chanced to come upon an old grave yard, that had gone into entire ruin. There could be seen the tombstone of the Revolutionary soldier, citizen and foreigner. The oldest one was dated 1727, that was the tombstone of an old lady sixty years old, and another of a president of his majesty's council in Virginia. He died in 1753, and all the rest of nearly the same date. It was a perfect pleasure to me to look over the old place, such a contrast to the clay hills of Manassas. I feel nearer home, but still I am a long ways off. I am wanted now, as they are continually detailing men for something or other. I will send the letter I wrote the other day. When the battle closes I will write again.

Give my love to all.

Your loving son,

GEORGE.[46]

P. S. I have not heard from Walter yet, except from a man that came from the hospital, he says that his hand is nearly well.

RICHMOND, VA., June 15, 1862.

Dear Mother:

I hope you are not uneasy about me because I have not written before. I knew if I wrote it would take a week for you to get it, so I put it off till I could send it by Mr. Albert Farmer,[47] who will go tomorrow. The Surgeon of the hospital has given me a passport to stay wherever I please in the city and report to him every week. I believe I should go crazy if I had to stay out in the hospital where everything is so dull and disheartening. In fact I don't believe I am the same being I was two weeks ago, at least I don't think as I used to and things don't seem as they did. I don't believe I will ever get over the death of George. The more I think of him the more it affects me, and unless I am in some battle and excitement I am eternally thinking of the last moments of his life. How he must have suffered, if he was conscious of it. I shall never forget it. I think a long letter from some of you would make me feel so much better. I shall send by Mr. Farmer my watch, sleeve buttons, also the shirt I wore off. Everything I ought to have left at home I brought away and a great many things I ought to have brought I left behind. I only brought one flannel shirt, and by the way I'll send this one back and try this summer without them, as they are very heavy for summer wear. The war news you read every day in the papers, but Capt. Billy Brown came down from Gordonville with some of Jackson's[48] prisoners. He says he was in Lynchburg. Twenty-two hundred were sent in and that thirteen hundred were on the way.

The Yankees that are near Richmond, we don't hear anything of, everything is quiet. Please some of you write me soon.

Your loving son,

WALTER.

My Dear Mother:

I am sorry I have kept you waiting so long before writing to you, but I thought I would wait until I could have a talk with General Anderson to find out what I was to do before writing. I sent word by John Hines,[50] also Dr. Barham,[51] that I was well and for them to tell you all the news. When I arrived at the Camp of our Regiment it was gone to Malvern Hill to have a fight with the Yankees. They did not return in a day or two. General Anderson went to Richmond immediately on business, so I did not have an opportunity of speaking with him until this morning. He was perfectly willing for me to come back into the office, so I commenced duty this morning. We have a very pleasant place for our quarters, a large two story house with plenty of shade, in an open field, where we have the breezes from every direction.

I don't know yet, but I may come up here to mess and sleep, though I thought I would wait a while. I haven't slept in a tent since I've been in camp, but once. That was last night. It rained yesterday morning, and the ground was wet, and the air rather cold, so I thought I would go in the tent, as it was convenient. I shall go in bathing tonight to cool off, and sleep out doors. We have an excellent place for that purpose, that is bathing. It's been awfully hot here today. I believe it is warmer here than at home.

General G. W. Smith was to-day assigned to the command of our Division. I understand he is an excellent officer. Some of our regiments in this brigade have received their conscripts. They are a very good looking set of men seen drilling in a field, as they were this morning. It looks right funny to see men so green, but I suppose all of us were so at first, and we ought not to make fun of them. Dossey's Regiment[52] is only about half mile from here. He has been to see me twice since I have been here. I went over to see him last Saturday. He was very well. I went up to see Dunham when I passed through Richmond, but he had gone home the week before, so I was disappointed. Give my best respects to all friends, and my love to all the family, some of you write often and tell me everything that happens about town.

Goodbye, as ever,

Your loving son,

WALTER

P. S. I've got to endorse this letter for the want of stamps. I haven't written any in so long a time that my hand is as stiff as if I had been mauling rails, you can readily see the difference now and some time ago. I hope it will soon get better.

I forgot to tell you that our whole brigade was throwing up breastworks every day, about two miles from here, that is the only duty they do now, no guard duty.

As You May Never See Us Again

My Dear Mother:

As Mr. Parker[53] will leave in the morning for home, I thought I would avail myself of the opportunity to let you hear from me. There is nothing new to write in the way of "War News." You hear everything that we do, and that's in the papers. Everything on our lines is quiet. We were put under marching orders a day or two ago, with the expectation of making another march to "Malvern Hill," but the Yankees left and it saved us the trouble of running them away. Eight hundred of the Brigade are still working on the breastworks, some two miles below here. I am in hopes the Yankees will never get near enough to Richmond for us to have to fight behind them. The other regiment in the Brigade has received their conscripts, ours is the smallest one and we haven't received a single one, and I hope we won't.

General Anderson was making a calculation this morning and he says that we have lost 226 men, killed and died from their wounds, since the day before we went into the fight at "Seven Pines."[54] The Regiment is now under command of Pat Simms. All of our company are in very good health. I don't believe that we have a single man on the sick list, and I believe it is owing in a great degree to the good water we get. It is the best we have had since we've been in Virginia. I am getting along very well indeed, enjoying excellent health, and have a very pleasant time.

We have very little writing to do, not half as much as we had at Manassas. General Anderson has no Adj. General yet. I would not be surprised if he was not waiting for Dunham to get well. I believe he likes Dunham better as an officer than any man in the Brigade. He has one of his brothers (Walker)[55] as one of his Aides. I wish you would please look in my trunk and send me that brown veil that you will find. I want it to put over my face when I take a nap in the morning, to keep off the flies. You never saw any flies yet, you can measure them by the bushel here. The mosquitoes are terrible here, too. I shall put it over my face when I sleep out of doors, and that's every night that it don't rain. I've just learned from Mr. Parker that little Leon[56] was dead. Poor little fellow, I never thought that when I left home it would be the last time I should see him.

Give my love to all the family, my respects to all my friends. Write soon, tell me all the news.

Your affectionate son,

WALTER

P. S. Please send the veil by the first one coming to our camp. Give my respects to all the boys that you see.

HEAD QUARTERS, ANDERSON BRIGADE,
30 MILES FROM RICHMOND ON MANASSAS
RAILROAD, August 23rd, 1862.

My Dear Mother:

This is the first opportunity that I have had to write to you since we left our camp near Richmond. Mr. Christman left us, or rather parted from us, in Richmond as we passed through on our march. Blake and myself did not get the barrel that was sent by Mr. Christman, though we had just as much fruit and Irish potatoes (that the company received) as we could eat. We left the very next morning after the night Mr. Christman arrived. The first day we marched about 14 miles and camped in an open field, the next day we march all day until dark. We stopped, ate our supper, spread our blankets and was just going to sleep, nearly every man exhausted, when the drum sounded and the order given for every man to be under arms. In ten minutes the brigade marched off and we continued the march until nearly day. The next morning, that is those that kept up, (the road for ten miles was strewn with men who had fallen out of ranks from exhaustion). We are now encamped at the place we arrived at that night. We have been here three days and it is impossible to tell when we will leave. This is a very important position for the Aides of General Jackson. The Yankees are about twelve miles from us and it was supposed that they would make an attack at this point, is the reason we were in such a hurry to get here that night. We would have made a very poor stand if they had. I don't suppose we had more than one third of the men when we arrived here that night, when we came through Richmond. I had a very good opportunity of judging as our company was detailed that day as a war guard of the Brigade, to prevent straggling, and I marched behind with them for company. It's no use trying to make a broken down man get up and march. We didn't know but what the Yankees were near or advancing on us, but the men would lie right down side of the road and swear they could not go one foot farther, Yankees or no Yankees. They are still coming in though it has been three days ago.

You may say what you please about marching twenty or thirty miles a day in warm weather, but I don't believe in it. The last day we marched twenty-six miles, we started at daylight and didn't stop until nearly day break the next morning, with about one third of the men, when we got to the end of our route, we had when we started and they were good for nothing, with their feet all blistered and sore. Mine have just got so I can walk without limping. You may direct your next letter to Richmond as heretofore, putting on the back "Smith's Division," and I reckon it will be forwarded. We have a very pleasant place to camp. I wouldn't care if we were to stay here for a month. General Anderson and his Staff are in tents at present, no house being near. Col. Grimes arrived this morning. The men are all very glad to see him return. They all love him since the fights that he has led them in. Give my love to all the family. Tell sister to write. I have writen, I believe, three letters home and haven't received but one.

Your affectionate son,

WALTER.

General Bryan Grimes

HEAD QUARTERS, ANDERSON'S BRIGADE,
SOUTH SIDE OF POTOMAC, OPPOSITE BERLIN,
LOUDON CO., Sept. 5, 1862.

My Dear Mother:

I guess you are all very anxious about me, that is to know my whereabouts. Since I last wrote you I have been through the most hardships that I ever have before. Today makes eleven successive days that we have been on the march, without resting a day since we left Anderson's station,[57] the place from which I last wrote you. We are now on the side south of the Potomac, opposite a place called Berlin, where there is some Yankees, don't know how many. We have our brigade and a tolerable good force of Artillery at this point. What we intend to do or where we are going, it's impossible to say. The men are all very anxious to drop over into Maryland and I don't know but what that will be our next move. We have just stopped for the night, after a march of about twenty miles. I'm in a hurry to finish before dark, as we have no candles or lightwood. Mr. Ed Marsh[58] will leave for North Carolina in the morning, he will carry our mail. We haven't had a chance to send off our mail before, since we waded the Rapidan River. Day before yesterday we marched over the battle ground that Jackson had his last fight on.[59] All of our men had been buried, but the Yankees lay just as they were killed. I never saw such a scene before. I saw just from the road, as I did not go out of my way to see any more. It must have been nearly a thousand. Our wagon actually ran over the dead bodies in the road before they would throw them out, or go around them. The trees were literally shot all to pieces. The wounded Yankees were all over the woods, in squads of a dozen or more, under some shady tree without any guard of any kind to guard them. I recollect one squad on the side of the road with their bush shelter in ten steps of a dead Yankee, that had not been buried and was horribly mangled. I don't suppose the dead Yankees of that fight will ever be buried.

Craig and Baker

It will be an awful job to those who do it, if it is ever done. There is some five or six of our company that have not come up yet. Blake is among the number. They are not sick, merely broken down. The Second N. C. Regiment[60] haven't more than half of the men with them now, that they had when they left Richmond. It has been an awfully hard march. Two men died in one day from sun stroke. The weather is not so warm now as some days ago. It takes two or three blankets to keep us warm at night, it is so cool. The days are very warm. I hope to gracious that we will stay here tomorrow and rest a while, it's a beautiful place on the side of the Blue Ridge. The sun will not strike the ground where our headquarters are during the whole day. I don't know where to tell you to direct your next letter. Richmond, though, I reckon. Give my love to all the family. Goodbye. I'll now cook my supper. I'll have an excellent one tonight, chicken, and sugar and coffee and biscuit.

Yours, etc.,

WALTER.

P.S. I bought sugar at 12 ½¢ per pound and coffee at 25¢ pound this morning in a store on our way.

HEAD QUARTER'S ANDERSON'S BRIGADE, MAR. BUNKER'S HILL,[61] VA., Sept. 29, 1862.

My Dear Mother:

It has been some time since I last wrote you. I hope you have not been uneasy about me, for I have never been in better health in my life. During the past two months we have been on the march almost constantly, sometimes resting one or two days, but never longer.

On Sunday, the 14th of September, we left our camp at 4 o'clock in the morning and marched some six miles to the top of the Blue Ridge and drew up in line of battle.[62] We were not long waiting for the Yankees, they came in very large columns and we fought until after dark. That night our troops fell back through Boonsboro[63] some few miles and drew up in line of battle little after sunrise, very little fighting was done on that day, only some cannonading. We continued in our position until the 17th inst., when we had almost a general engagement. The line of battle of our Brigade was some two hundred yards in front of a house in which General D. H. Hill[64] and General Anderson had their Head Quarters. The fight commenced in the morning before I awoke (long before sunrise), soon after light the wounded from the Artillery commenced coming in, pretty soon the wounded infantry came in by the dozens. There wasn't a surgeon on the battle field from our Brigade, but Gus Stith.[65] He stayed there to the last. He, his two assistants and myself dressed the wounds until the Yankees got in 30 yards of the house. General Anderson was anxious to get off before the Yankees got nearer. He did not want to be taken prisoner by them. He would prefer being shot through the head, so Capt. Gales,[66] his A. A. General, myself and two other men of the Ambulance Corps carried him through a field that looked like it was impossible for man to walk ten steps without being killed, though we got out safe. A piece of shell struck me on the knee, which occasioned some little inconvenience for a

Craig and Baker

few days, but nothing else. The house in which we were was the hottest part of the battle field, we were exposed to a cross fire of two Yankee Batteries and from the front by musket balls. The house, kitchen, trees and everything else was torn and shot all to pieces. We had a large pot full of chicken on the stove, cooking for dinner, when a bomb took off one-half of the kitchen and turned the stove bottom upwards. That stopped the splendid dinner we had in preparation. You must get Gus Stith to tell you all about our campaign, adventures, etc. He can do it better than I can write it. Every day's march through Maryland I could write a long letter, but when it is all past and forgotten I can't think of one thing that I wished to write. If I ever live to get home I can think of one thing at a time, and tell you a great many little incidents of interest. The Northern part of Virginia and some parts of Maryland is the most beautiful country that I ever saw. I don't know how it is in the winter, but from the looks of the soil, it's as muddy as Manassas, I reckon. We (our company) lost several in the two battles, none killed, but some badly wounded, others taken prisoners or have not come up yet, may be wounded and left on the battlefield and had to be left in the hands of the Yankees when we fell back this side of the Potomac. We are now encamped on the Turnpike from Martinsburg to Winchester, some ten miles from the latter place.

I don't know where to tell you to direct your next letter, Richmond, though, I reckon. Our mail for this Brigade is at Winchester, we will get that to-day. I hope to get some letters from home when it comes. I must close this so as to have it ready when Gus Stith starts, he can't tell when, so I must have it ready. I may get something in the mail before this gets off.

Your loving son,

WALTER

NEAR BUNKER HILL, VA., October 1st, 1862.

Dear Mother:

I have just received a letter from you, dated Sept. 2nd. It is the first word I have heard from home since I left Richmond (I forgot I did receive one letter down at Anderson's station, 30 miles from Richmond). It appears that you have not received the letter I wrote from the Potomac, opposite Berlin, though you must have gotten it before now. I heard that Pat Simms will be in Wilson for a short time as detail for our winter clothing. He can tell you all about that trip. It has been so long that I have forgotten almost all about it. I shall send this by Dr. Stith, as he starts in the morning. You can get him to tell you a good deal of news if you choose. Dr. Stith and Pat Wooten[67] came up this morning. I haven't been up to see them yet. I must sleep and stay at head quarters nearly all the time, as it is more convenient and I get plenty of something to eat, and often something extra. If Pat Simms goes home, as I think he will, you may send me my two flannel shirts and my drawers, also two pair of woolen socks. I reckon I will have to make out with shoes this winter, though if you can have me a good pair of winter sewed boots made (large 6s) you may send them also, and the price. If I can't wear them myself I can sell them for any price I may choose to ask. See if Pat is willing to bring them first and if he is certain that he can get them here without being lost. Write often by some of the boys that are coming.

Your affectionate son,

WALTER

HEAD QUARTERS, ANDERSON'S BRIGADE,
November 14, 1862.

My Dear Mother:

As I have another good opportunity of sending a letter the other side of Richmond to be mailed, I thought I would avail myself of it. One of our surgeons will leave in the morning for North Carolina, so that I can have my letter mailed very near home, it will stand less chance of being lost. I have neglected to write to you longer than I wished, waiting for an opportunity of sending it by some one. This is the first chance that has occurred. The letters that are mailed here for North Carolina, not one half of them ever get there, so I made up my mind not to write except when I knew you would receive it. We have been through a good many hardships since I last wrote to you, tho' we haven't had any fighting, that is, our Brigade has not, tho' we have lain in line of battle several days and nights at the time, waiting for the advance of the enemy. The strongest position I think our Division ever occupied was on the mountains behind rock fences, near Paris.[68] We stayed there one day and night, but the Yankees didn't come. We left there and marched to Port Royal,[69] there we laid in line of battle two days and one night. Little after dark the second day we got orders to cross the Shenandoah River and take up camp some mile or two off for the night. The men were cold and hungry and somewhat expecting the Yankees that night, when the word was given they started at a double quick for the river, some half mile off, and in they went, half waist deep, the water was freezing cold and the wind almost cutting you in two. I guess you know something about the mountain winds in the winter. For the next few days we had some rest, but we don't lie idle in camp long at a time. Night before last we marched seven miles, tore up and burned railroads all night, and marched back ten miles the next day. To-day is a beautiful sunshiny one, and I hope we will remain quiet for the men's sake. We have had one snow some two or three inches deep, though it melted very soon, there are thousands of barefooted men in Virginia and I do hope we will have pleasant weather until they can get shoes. We have a good many in our Brigade stark barefooted, and have not had a shoe on since we left Richmond some months ago. John Burton,[70] poor fellow, was paroled and came up with us some week or two back, looking dreadfully. He has gone home on a furlough. He was barefooted and almost clothesless. My feet can just be said to be off the ground and that is all. They are no protection from wet weather. I hope Pat Simms will come soon and have my boots with him. I am glad you sent me a pair of pants, as these are entirely worn out. I have been patching them up for some time. There is two big patches on the knees as large as your two hands, put on with blue cloth, you recollect the pants are brown. I never thought to mention any clothes in my letter. I hope you thought of them. I need a pair. I also need an overcoat, but I will have to wait until the Regiment get their clothes before I can get one. I hope before one month more passes we will be on the railroad somewhere, so I can get something good to eat once more. I think I will know how to appreciate something good after living on beef and bread for so long. I want some oysters and sweet potatoes and other winter delicacies so much. I hope, if we ever do get where I can change my diet, I will be able to stop the diarrhoea which has been reducing me for some time. I've fallen off considerable since we left Richmond. With that exception I have nothing to complain of. In a great many respects I fare a great deal better than the officers of the regiment do. I have better fare and not half the duty to do.

The other night, when all the men were at work on the railroad, I was with our wagon and had as comfortable a night's sleep as I ever do. I very often get a chance to ride on the march, too, for the last several marches I have ridden Col. Grimes' extra horse. Since we left Richmond we have crossed twenty streams waist deep and very often in the night, and I have never waded

Craig and Baker

one yet. I always get a ride across, some way or another.

We will have a general change at Headquarters in a few days. General Ramseur is assigned to this Brigade and I expect he will bring his own Staff with him. I'll stand as good a chance of remaining as any of them and I think I will be very apt to remain, at least I shall try to do so. I hope he will be as clever as the other commanders have been. I like Col. Grimes very much and I think he is more entitled to the promotion of Brigadier than Ramseur, who was only a Captain of Artillery, though they say he is a West Pointer, and a very good officer. I hope he will prove himself to be as good as General Anderson was, though that is hardly possible. I don't think he had his equal in the Confederate Army. I hope Dr. Harrell will pass his examination and get in the army as surgeon. It is the easiest and most comfortable position there is in the Army.

Tell Mr. Rhodes if I was in his place I would try and get in a new company, one that has not been in long. Dr. Bullock's[71] Company would suit him better than any other. He thinks that we've got a good one and a picked company, but it is not what it was, and he would be out of place all the time if he would try to keep up with men who had been playing the old soldier for nearly two years. I would rather be dead than in the place of some of the Conscripts sent to our Regiment, they look like they wanted to die, they felt so bad. Please let me know in your next whether you ever received my watch or not. I've asked in every letter and you've never told me yet. Write soon to your

Affectionate son,
WALTER

P.S. Give my love to all the family, tell some of them to write. I haven't sent a letter home yet with a stamp on it, it is because we can't possibly get them and I know it makes no difference with you.

HEADQUARTERS FOURTH BRIGADE.
November 27, 1862.

My Dear Mother:

I received your letter yesterday, and also one from brother by Mr. Gorman.[72] I was very glad to hear from you, as I had not received any news from home in some time. He handed me the gloves also, which you sent by him. Nothing ever came in better time in the world. I had been trying my best to get a pair of some kind ever since cold weather set in, but could not, gloves such as you sent me sell for $3.00 in this country, and everything else in proportion. The last letter that I wrote home, sent to Richmond by Capt. John Grimes[73] to be mailed, was from our Camp near Strasburg, Va.[74] We left there on Friday, the 21st, and arrived here on Tuesday evening, the 25th, making a march of over one hundred miles in four days. It is the best marching that we have ever done, it's because we are going towards home, I reckon, that the men did so well. There are hundreds of them barefooted and ice on the ground all day. General Hill[75] issued an order yesterday requiring all the barefooted men to make sandals of raw hides with the hair on the inside. It answers the purpose very well. It's a wonder the idea had not been thought of sooner, before the men suffered so much. Gorman says that Pat Simms will be here to-day with the things for the Regiment. I hope he will be, for I need my boots very badly, also my pants. I shall draw a pair of pants from the Regimental clothing, also a pair of shoes. I bought me a Yankee overcoat, a very comfortable one, for $12.50, a better coat than our men draw at more money. We are now on our way to Hanover Junction,[76] some fifty miles off. We have stopped here to transport our sick on the cars ahead of us, though we have been here going on two days, a longer time than would be required for that purpose. We have no idea how long we will stay here. From what you write about your exchanging farms, I think you made a very good bargain. I wish I could be with you to help

you fix it up. The boys are all well as could be expected. Virgil Stevens looks thin from diarrhoea. Tom Stith looks as fat as a pig. Buck Hansill is the same old "Buck," though Marshbourns, that is Sam, is well and tough, Jim I don't recollect having seen for some time. I really don't know whether he is in the company or not. I did write to you and intended to send it by Ed Gordon, but he left just before I carried my letters up to the Company to give him. The next time any one leaves Wilson for the Company, please send me some kind of tonic bitters. I need something of the kind.

Give my love to all, and believe me as ever,

Your affectionate son,

WALTER

HEAD QUARTERS FOURTH BRIGADE,
HILL'S DIV., NEAR GUINEA DEPOT,
12 MILES FROM FREDERICKSBURG,
December 2nd., 1862.

My Dear Mother:

Once more settled in camp for a little while, long enough to
write, at least, I thought I would let you know where we are and
what we are doing. We are on the railroad between Richmond and
Fredericksburg, some twelve miles from the latter place. What
we are doing, one hasn't the remotest idea. We can't tell whether
we are going to fight here or not, or how long we shall stay here.
I think the most of our army is in this vicinity and some part of
it is constantly in motion. Ewell's Division[77] is now passing our
encampment. I'm in hopes we will stay here until our men get
their clothing. Ed Gordon has just returned, though he does not
bring any news from home. He says that Pat Simms will start
back to-day. He certainly has appointed enough times for starting
to have been here long before now, if he is not able to bring the
things, why doesn't he let some one else come with them. The
men have been kept out of their clothing long enough. May Warren, I understand, is willing to bring them. If you should receive
this before any of them leaves, please send my watch and chain
by him, I need the use of it very much and I don't think there
is any danger of my losing it or being killed this winter or fall,
campaign is about over. If both of them have left, please send it
by the first reliable person coming to our company. Please have a
key fitted to it and send that also, also a piece of buckskin in my
trunk. Wrap them all up together and enjoin the one that brings
it to be very careful with it, and not to lose it. I have not time to
write much more, as Major Miller,[78] who is going to take my letter
to Richmond to be mailed, is in a hurry to go to the depot, for
fear of being left. I received the things which you sent by Buck
Hansill, also the gloves you sent by John Gorman, all I need now

Craig and Baker

are the things which you are going to send by Pat Simms. Give my love to all the family and believe me, as ever, your

Affectionate son,

WALTER

P. S. Write often and tell me all the news about home. Wrap my watch up very securely and direct it to me. Don't forget to send me a key for it, as I have none.

My Dear Mother:

As I think there will be an opportunity of sending off a letter in a day or two, I believe I will drop you a few lines to let you know of some of my adventures since I last wrote you (Winchester). We have had rain every day since we left Winchester. I've been marching about ten to twenty miles a day. After the first two days our squad of two hundred dwindled down to about fifteen men, most of whom were officers. A Lieutenant from Texas commanded us. We were bound to form squads of some strength to prevent "bushwhackers" and the enraged citizens from attacking us on the road. Last summer was nothing at all to this one in Pennsylvania. Although I did not have the pleasure of going into Yankeeland with them, I was following them in the rear and could see the havoc they did. The squad that I was in, the first night we got into Pennsylvania, killed a hog near a man's house and then sent two men to him to borrow cooking utensils to cook it in, most of them would make the expression, "I reckon you got your rations out of the field."

The Fourth of July we got in eight miles of the battlefield, all that day the citizens tried their best to prevent our going any farther. Told us we were certainly gone chickens if we went any farther, that the Yankees were on picket some little distance off in large force. We didn't put any confidence in their chat but kept on. The last day of the three days' big fight, we got within a few miles of the battlefield, when we met General Imboden's Cavalry, the advance guard of our whole wagon train, who turned us back by orders from General Lee, ordering us at the same time to keep with the train, which did not stop until we arrived at this place, we (the wagon train) intended to ford the river here and again set foot on Virginia soil, but it has rained so much we have been waiting four days for the river to fall low enough to ford it. The Yankees attacked us here day before yesterday with the intention of capturing us, but they were driven off. I can't form the most distant idea what the army is going to do, whether they intend to stay this side of the river or go back into Virginia. There is not a day passes but you hear of fighting going on. You don't feel right unless you hear cannonading going on. The stillness doesn't seem natural. There are five or six thousand Yankees here waiting for the river to fall to cross.

When I have more time I will write again. Captain Thompson was wounded slightly and has crossed the river, I don't know with what intention. Buck Nolly[80] was killed in our company.

Write to me as soon as you get this and let me hear from you all, direct to Richmond and I will get it. This letter is No. 3.

WALTER

CAMP NEAR ORANGE C. H., August 2nd, 1863

My Dear Mother:

I received your letter day before yesterday, just as we received orders to march. We marched about fifteen miles yesterday through the hottest sun that I ever felt. The men were constantly dropping out from overheat, and one or two died from the effects. We are in camp to-day, but have orders to hold ourselves in readiness to move at a moment's notice. The report is the Yankees are advancing on Culpepper.[81] I guess we will leave here tonight or before day in the morning. This army is seeing a very hard time at present. Nothing to eat but beef and flour and the hardest marching that this army has ever done. At the time we crossed the mountains at Port Royal, we marched from 4 o'clock one morning until day break next morning. We were drawn up in line of battle twice during the time, once we had a very sharp fight between our sharpshooters and the Yankees. Our Brigade was in line on an edge of a mountain overlooking the whole scene. I don't think it will be long before we shall have a fight, from our present movements. I thought I told you in the letter I wrote from near Hargerstown, while in line, that I was with the Regiment. You must have missed getting that letter. This makes the fifth I have written since I left home. When I got with the regiment everything had so much changed at headquarters, new men detailed, and my not knowing any of them, I concluded to go back with the company. I have been doing duty with the Company ever since I got back and I believe I feel better satisfied. Jim Gay[82] got back to the regiment this morning, left Wilson last Wednesday. He has told us all about the Yankee raid.

I have been suffering some little from pain in the feet, caused by hard marching. The doctor told me yesterday that I might put my things in the ambulance. At night when I went after them, some one had stolen my knapsack with all my clothes, except what I have on, and my shawl. I'll try and make out with what

I have until cold weather comes on. You may send me two pair cotton and two pair woolen socks the first opportunity you have. That will be the first thing that I will need. Dossey came over to see me this morning and read a letter to me that he got from Cousin Claudia yesterday.

There is some little talk sometimes of our Brigade being ordered to North Carolina. I wish to gracious we could be. I'll bet the Yankees wouldn't cut up there like they have been. To-day is Sunday and one of the hottest that I ever felt. We are in a piece of woods where there isn't one breath of air stirring. If we do have to march to-day, half of the men will give out from over-heat. I would much rather march two nights than one day. You may send me that homespun shirt in my trunk, at the same time you do the socks — that checked one. I hope the authorities will send some troops home to prevent the Yankees from making a raid through there. Write whenever there is anything to tell me about home and you all.

Your affectionate son,

WALTER.

My Dear Mother:

I had intended to write you the very day we left Orange Court House, but the movement prevented me. We left there yesterday week, marched towards Rapidan, camped near the river for two days, hearing the cannonading between our forces and the Yankees the whole time, neither crossing in any force. Our cavalry made a dash across the river, taking some thirty prisoners. The Second North Carolina Cavalry are on the other side of the river now and is thought to be cut off. We are now eighteen miles from Orange Court House on the Rapidan river. I can't learn the name of the ford. Our division is in line of battle, about one mile from the river. We have thrown up some breastworks and we have an excellent position. All I hope is that the Yankees may come across, for I feel confident we can whip them worse than they have ever been yet. A deserter who came across says they have only two corps and that they are most conscripts. He says they are deserting by the hundreds. Last evening our division moved in a piece of woods some three hundred yards in rear of our breastworks. I suppose it was done that the men might keep more comfortable. Night before last we had a pretty smart frost and the wind blew like winter. I spent two thirds of the night by the fire to keep warm. My pair of blankets got left in one of the wagons.

If you do not have any use for that map of Virginia, which you bought last winter, please loan it to me; send it by Thompson. I will take good care of it and return it.

In times like this, one blanket is as much as any man wants hung to him, and nine times out of ten he throws that one away during the fight. As soon as we go into camp again I shall have plenty of bedding. When Dr. Thompson comes back, I wish you would send my overcoat. I think I shall need it by then, also one

Craig and Baker

pair of woolen socks. The flannel drawers you may keep until we go into camp. I have no way of carrying them. I never intend to carry another knapsack on my back, as long as I stay in the service. John Valentine[83] brought the things you sent by him. The shirt fits exactly. You need not trouble about making the other in any hurry. I shall not need it until we go in camp.

Henry Warren came to us yesterday morning. The bag of potatoes which he brought could not have come in a better time. It was a rich treat, I assure you. We have been lying in line of battle two or three days, living on half cooked rations sent from the wagon yard, and to get a bag of sweet potatoes was a perfect Godsend. We just set around the fire and roasted them last night and talked of the good things at home for a late hour. Tom Stith, Tom Atkinson,[84] Peter Christman and myself compose our mess and whatever either gets, he shares it with the rest. Tom Stith has a trunk of things at Orange Court House, that Henry had to leave, as he had to take it afoot to where he found us; his boy brought my potatoes. Tell sister that I will write to her soon. I should have written this time, but couldn't get the paper. It took me half an hour to borrow this half sheet. You need not look for me home on a furlough for a long time yet; there are men in the camp that haven't been home since we came to Virginia. You know I have been home twice. It will be a long time before my time comes around. The next furlough, I expect, will be a wounded or sick one.

Give my love to all the family and believe me as ever,

Your affectionate son,

WALTER.

CAMP NEAR MORTON'S FORD,[85]
ON RAPIDAN RIVER, October 5th, 1863.

My Dear Mother:

I received your letter of the 23rd yesterday while on picket duty and it seems to me from the way in which you write that you did not receive my last letter. I don't think that it has been two weeks since I wrote you; 'twas soon after Harry Warren got back. We are at the same camp we were when Henry came. Our Brigade does picket on the river at Morton's Ford. We (that is, our Regiment) have to go on every fourth night. Night before last was a terrible night, cold and rainy, and the wind was pretty cutting. Our line is on the river bank, in a cornfield. The Yankees are on the other side, some four hundred yards distance. We have no communication with them, it being against General Ramseur's orders. Battle's Brigade[86] (Alabama troops) talk and exchange papers with them every day. They join our line above the ford. When we first went on picket at the river we could hear the Yankees' drums by the hundred. They stopped all at once and we did not hear more than two or three for a whole week. Yesterday morning they opened with their drums again and from the number it would seem that they have a large army across the river. I think they tried to make us believe they had left, but they can't fool General Lee. We have had orders for a week or more to keep two days' rations cooked and be ready to move at a moment's notice. I don't think that we shall remain much longer at this camp.

Some half-dozen cannons were heard up the river yesterday. I suppose they were signal guns. A pretty good sign of a movement. I hope we will soon do all the fighting that we expect to do this winter, and let us go into winter quarters. The orderly has just come around with orders to be in readiness to move, as the Yankees are advancing and we may probably leave this evening. All the preparation that I have to make is to look up our day's rations of bread. As soon as we go into camp to stay any length of time, I shall be glad to get my flannel drawers. I will let you know. I hope Dr. Thompson will be well enough to come when his furlough is out, and bring my overcoat, also a pair of socks, gloves (if you can find them) and a little box of lip salve. Tom Stith was waiting about a week before he got his things, which Henry Warren brought. He had to leave them at Orange Court House, as he had to foot it about eighteen miles. Col. Grimes got back a few days ago from North Carolina. He was married while home and he is now a candidate for congress, and I think he will probably be elected. I would like very much to be at home with you to eat some of that nice fruit which you have. Peaches here in camp sell for $2.00 per dozen, so we can't afford to eat as many as we want at that price, or it would take a month's wages to pay for the treat. Blake said for me to tell you to please tell Mr. Rhodes to send him thirty dollars by Thompson, if this reaches you in time; if not, send it by mail. Tom Stith says to tell some of his folks not to send him any blanket as yet. He will let them know.

I am enjoying excellent health at present. Sometimes I am troubled with diarrhoea, but I generally stop it by quit eating beef for a few days. Next time you write to Pussy,[87] give her my best love and tell her I would like so much to see her. Give my love to all the family, and believe me, your sincere and devoted son,

WALTER

P.S. Much obliged for the paper and envelopes.

ON MARCH NEAR RAPPAHANNOCK STATION, VA.,[88]
October 18, 1863.

My Dear Mother:

I received your very welcome letter and did intend answering it last evening, but we were ordered to move, which prevented me from doing so. We left Rapidan about the 7th inst., and have been on the march ever since, and I believe it has been the hardest for the length of time that we have ever had. It was what might be termed a "flank movement" in every sense of the word. We marched through woods, fields and across branches, creeks and rivers as we came to them, only a few hours behind the Yankees all the time. Last Thursday we were drawn up in line of battle before day and our Division, with our sharpshooters in front, drove the Yankees through the woods and fields for two or three miles. Our sharpshooters killed and wounded a great many. Our Brigade took thirty or forty prisoners. A day or two before that we surprised a corps of Yankees in camp, hurrying them off rather unceremoniously. We all got our haversacks filled with crackers, which we very much needed, though we haven't suffered for anything to eat on the march. Gen. Ramsieur is very attentive to his men in that respect. Day before yesterday we were in four miles of Manassas. I did wish that we might go that far. I wanted to see the old place so much.

The rumor in camp is that Gen. Lee has accomplished everything he intended, that is, to drive the Yankees back and tear up this railroad, which we are doing to perfection; but for the grading and bent iron you would not know that there ever was a railroad along here. We cut down the telegraph wire also, and carried that along with us. We stopped on the march to-day, about 10 o'clock, after marching about eight miles. What it is for, I can't tell. I suppose something is the matter with the road ahead, or probably the bridge across the Rappahannock needs repairing. It is now 4 o'clock. I expect we shall move nearer the river to camp, however it does not make much difference where we stop, as we have rations up till tomorrow evening. I wish you could have seen us cooking up three days' rations the other night, before attacking the Yankees the next day. We have flour and beef to cook and only about half the night to cook them in, without cooking utensils. We made up our dough on our gun cloths and cooked it on barrel staves and heads. You would be surprised to see how nice bread can be cooked on a ram rod. I think it is the sweetest bread that I ever ate. I think there must be something in the appetite also. Our beef we broiled on griddle irons made of telegraph wire. I think I was the first in our regiment to make one; since then nearly every man has one along with him. Col. Grimes detailed a blacksmith and sent him to me to get mine to make him one like it. He said it was the most useful thing he had seen. We cook bread on them also. Speaking of Col. Grimes, he just received a furlough to-day, and will leave for North Carolina in a few days. Dr. Thompson has not arrived yet, nor have we heard from him. I think the fall campaign is about over and I hope we will go into winter quarters somewhere on the railroad. I do want some sweet potatoes so much. Give my love to all the family, and believe me as ever,

Your devoted son,
WALTER.

P. S. I am truly glad that Dr. Harrell has got a position as surgeon. I hope he will be pleasantly situated. Please look in the watch pocket of my black satin vest, get my lip salve box, fill it with salve and send it in your next letter. This mountain wind keeps my lips split all to pieces. Tell Mr. Rhodes, Blake says he got the $30.00 safely; much obliged to him. I believe I will send you a Yankee letter that I picked up the other day in the woods while we were pursuing them. I don't think peace is so near at hand as he does. Much obliged for this envelope and paper, you got an answer sooner than you otherwise would, there is no sutler along with us and none of the boys carry such things with them, they cost so much, and the first rain would ruin them.

November 11th, 1863.

My Dear Mother:

We are once more in our same camp on the Rapidan, which we left just a month ago. We had just begun to be comfortable in our winter quarters on the Rappahannock when the Yankees run us out. Last Saturday, about ten o'clock, the Yankees attacked our picket line on the river, composed of the Second and Thirtieth N. C. Regiments of our Brigade, driving them back, taking a great many of them prisoners. Col. Cox,[89] of the Second, was badly wounded and afterwards died. The attack was a perfect surprise.

We had just drawn a large supply of winter clothing of every kind, and the men were just trying them on when we were ordered to fall in, which we did in double quick time, making for the river line of battle with our sharpshooters in front. 'Twas not long before we came on their skirmishers and a brisk fire commenced, which lasted until dark. Our two lines of battle laid within speaking distance until 12 o'clock that night, when we were very quietly withdrawn, half hour afterwards our sharpshooters followed and we took up our line of march till sun rise, when we were drawn up in line of battle, we stayed until two or three o'clock. The Yankees not coming on us, we started on the march again and never stopped till we crossed the Rapidan. We ate our breakfast Saturday morning in our winter quarters and did not draw a single mouthful to eat, or have any rest except when we were in line of battle (and then we were hard at work throwing up breastworks), until Monday night, ten o'clock. We waded the Rapidan about 9 o'clock the same night. I think it was the hardest time we have ever had, nothing to eat, accompanied with the hardest marching we ever did. All of our things were left in our winter quarters, expecting to go back there, but we did not, so we lost a good many things which we left behind. I happened to take my shawl and oil cloth along with me, which I saved. I lost

Craig and Baker

my two blankets, a pair of cotton drawers, pair of socks, which I had just drawn (I did not draw anything else of the new clothing, which I am glad of, for I should have lost them). I also lost my knapsack, tin plate, tin cup, etc. I saved my overcoat, with all the things you sent by Condon.[90] That scrape has taught me a lesson. I'll bet I never leave anything else of mine behind. I don't care where we are ordered to.

Try and get Tom Stith to put the following things in with his own baggage: That worsted shirt, flannel shirt, flannel drawers, two pair socks, please send me a comb, coarse one, also a towel. Tom Stith will be judge of what he can bring besides those things. Tell him we are at the same camp that Henry Warren came to us at. If I have time I will write to him tomorrow. We have just as much to do now as we can attend to. We are on picket every third night (Nov. 12). We moved camp this morning about half mile nearer our picket line. Cannonading is occasionally heard on the other side of the river. I don't know what we will be doing, or where we will be tomorrow this time. I am perfectly willing for the Yankees to cross here, for I think we will whip them worse than we ever did at Fredricksburg. I shall be on picket tonight. I've got to go to work and get something to eat to carry with me. Give my love to all. As ever,

Your sincere and devoted son,

WALTER.

CAMP NEAR MORTON'S FORD, VA.,
December 3rd, 1863.

My Dear Mother:

I know you are anxious to hear from me, so I thought I would write, if not but a few lines, to let you hear from me and to know that I was well and safe. We left this place to-day was one week ago. That night at 3 o'clock we left and went down the river towards Germanna Ford,[91] where the Yankees have crossed in heavy force. We got there late in the evening, and had some very sharp skirmishes with them before night. We were in line of battle all night; just before day we fell back a short distance and established our line of battle and commenced throwing up our breastworks in the coldest kind of a rain. We were in an old field on top of a hill, where the wind came with all its fury. The smoke from our fires was almost enough to kill a man. We were in that condition, expecting an attack by the Yankees day or night. We have to keep all of our things on all the time and one-half of the men up all night, in case of an attack. Yesterday morning we commenced moving about 2 o'clock, and at daylight we discovered that the Yankees had retreated across the river. Our Brigade was ordered to the front and we commenced the pursuit. We pretty soon commenced taking a few stragglers and by ten o'clock we have taken (from the looks of them as we passed them on the road this morning) three or four hundred. They were the poorest Yankees I ever saw. They did not have one mouthful to eat and said they had not had any in four days. They stated as an excuse that our cavalry had captured their wagons. Several of them offered me $2.00 a piece for crackers, but I told them we were rationed up for two days and I could eat everything in my haversack in one, so I could not spare them. I told them that they would draw something to eat pretty soon.

One of them gave me his knapsack and everything in it and then very politely asked me if I could spare him a cracker. I could

Craig and Baker

not refuse him, for the things that he gave me unsolicited were very valuable. A pair of new shoes and a Yankee tent are things that money will not buy. I would not take $25.00 for my tent which he gave me. They are large enough for two, and so light that you can roll them in your knapsack and not feel the weight at all. I could have gotten more little Yankee camp conveniences than I could carry, but we were then in line of battle, charging through the woods and I did not wish to bungle myself up too much. I do not know how long we shall stay here, but it's my opinion, not long. I hope it will be long enough for us to get rested and recruited again before we set out for another march. Tom Stith brought all the things which you sent by him, including the letters. I am too tired and worn out to write an interesting letter. I merely wrote to set your mind at ease. As soon as I can cook something I shall try and go to sleep. I haven't slept more than an hour at any time for nearly a week. My love to all. Write soon to your

Sincere and affectionate son,

WALTER.

My Dear Mother:

I received your letter by mail, also the one you sent by Mixson. We were on picket at the time. Mixson[92] got here to-day (Sunday) week. We got back from picket last night, having spent one week on the banks of the Rapidan. We had two snows during the time, each one two or three inches deep. Though we did not suffer as one would suppose, who does not know how to fix up. My little Yankee tent came into requisition, so did my visor; you can't imagine the comfort there is in it while exposed to cold north winds. I thought I had written to you how I liked it. I used to think I wouldn't wear one, now I wouldn't be without it for anything. You say you wish I was in the office again. I do not. Though I was never allowanced while there for something to eat, there were other things equally as disagreeable. I get enough to eat now, but none to waste and I feel much better satisfied. Our meat has been cut down to a quarter of a pound and they give us sugar, coffee, rice and sometimes dried fruit. We eat up everything they give us and feel hungry all the time. When they only give us a quarter of a pound of meat and a tin cupful of flour, it is not enough for a hearty man, but when they give us rice, peas, etc., we can make out very well. Peter Christman got a letter from his father yesterday, saying he was going to start with a load of boxes to-day (Sunday) week. I suppose he will come in May Warren's place. I need not tell you what to send me, for I know you will be certain to send me as much as I could ask for. I don't wish for you to send me anything that is scarce or high priced. Let it be something that you have a plenty of, so that you will not miss it. The things that you sent by Mixson came in a very good time. He sent me some meat and potatoes while on picket. You can send me a little of that nice meal, if you have it to spare. You need not send any sage, just send a few pods of red peppers to

Craig and Baker

boil with beef once in a while, when we draw it. I don't suppose we shall draw much more beef until next Spring. Please don't forget to send a small case knife, a fig stem for pipe, the size of your middle finger, about six inches long.

I am very well supplied with winter clothing of every kind at present. Just drawn a splendid pair of English shoes. The trip down the river cut my others all to pieces. I did want to send a pair of English shoes to brother, but it seems that I can't get ahead so that I can do so. If we didn't have any picket duty to do this winter, we should be just as comfortable as I could wish. But we have to go eight miles off every fifth week and spend the time out doors, don't make any difference what kind of weather it is. I don't suppose we shall have to go more than two or three times, though before we shall start on our next Spring's campaign, wherever that may be. Tell Bob[93] to write whenever you do and let me know how he is getting along himself. Give my love to all the family, also to Puss whenever you write to her. Write as soon as is convenient and believe me, as ever,

Your sincere and affectionate son,

WALTER.

CAMP FOURTH NORTH CAROLINA REG'T.,
NEAR ORANGE COURT HOUSE, Jan. 26, 1864

My Dear Folks:

Your letter of the 16th inst. received a few days ago. Mr. Christman and the boxes got here Sunday night. Everything came safely, with the exception of Tom Stith's box, that got stolen passing through Richmond; the practiced thieves around Richmond can steal anything.

You can't tell how I prize that middling[94] of meat. It came in the very nick of time. I had just finished the ham and sausages which you sent by Nixson. The things which you have sent me will last me several weeks; with what I draw will give me just as much as I want by mixing rations. You don't know how selfish men become by soldiering two or three years. Two years ago when one received a box from home he was expected to ask the whole company up and tell them to help themselves, but that custom has played out. Now when a fellow buys anything or has anything sent him from home, the rest of the company don't expect to be asked to help themselves. Whoever one is messing with he is all that expects to share it with him; the whole company is messed off in pairs to suit themselves. I have been messing with Lang Mixson since we left Morton's Ford. He is the best messmate I have ever had. I will never mess with more than one at a time again. When two are together it enables them to cook and draw the rations for each other, when either is on duty. Mr. Winstead, our orderly, will leave in the morning for home. I shall send this by Wm. Barnes, who will leave with Mr. Christman. Give my love to all.

Yours,

WALTER.

CAMP NEAR ORANGE COURT HOUSE, VA.,
February 8, 1864.

Dear Mother:

I received your letter last week and I had just commenced to answer it when I heard commotion at Morton's Ford. Our Brigade was on picket last week, one week sooner than our time, in consequence of Gen. Battle's and Johnston's Brigades[95] having gone somewhere, I suppose to North Carolina. I was on camp guard at the time and was left for camp duty. Our Brigade had fallen in to start back to camp when our cannon on picket fired into the Yankees then graping. Before the boys could get to the breastworks, the Yankees had driven the picket line into them. They kept up a pretty sharp skirmish for three or four hours. The sharpshooters got so near to each other that they run and shot each other around a house, one Yankee was killed on the piazza of the house. There was only one man in our Brigade that was hurt, his name was W. A. Driver,[96] belonging to our company. He was wounded on the skirmish line. The Yankees lost some ten or fifteen. We killed one of their Generals, but they succeeded in getting him across the river. That night our line of pickets were posted in their same old posts. We heard here in camp that the Yankees were about to take our breastworks.

Next morning, Sunday, Peter Christman and myself rolled up our things and by daylight were on our way to the breastworks. When we got there our army was lying in our breastworks and the Yankees were scattered all over the fields about a half-mile the other side of the river. All their cannons were in position and remained so during the day. There were two lines of artillery just the right distance from each other to do the best execution, frowning at each other the whole day, neither willing or inclined to commence the fight across the river.

Last night about ten o'clock, their camp fires all died out and this morning the Yankees were all gone, except their line of pickets.

We pretty soon started back to camp and got here an hour ago, and I am in hopes they will not trouble us any more this winter. The mountains in Yankeedom were covered with snow this morning. I am in hopes we will have some shortly to put an end to all military operations for this winter. I will write again in a day or two. I am as tired as a horse at present, a tramp of ten miles through the mud ankle deep is enough to tire a mule. Give love to all.

As ever, your devoted son,

WALTER.

Craig and Baker

CAMP, FOURTH N. C., NEAR ORANGE COURT
HOUSE, February, 1864

My Dear Mother:

I received your letter dated February 21st, Friday, and I should have answered it yesterday, but for the want of time. Our Brigade has about one mile of plank road to ditch and grade and there is a very heavy detail from the Regiment every day. The whole regiment is on duty every day and will be for eight or ten days more. Those that are not on guard are at work on the roads. I came off guard this morning and will be on fatigue duty tomorrow until we make some move. We got orders this morning to cook up two days' rations and keep it on hand until further orders. I can't imagine what it is for. We have had so much nice weather for the past week or two. I think our General anticipates an attack. I don't like the idea of leaving our winter quarters this time of the year. We are bound to have some very severe weather yet. The day Cullen[97] left, it snowed about two or three inches deep, and before the next day at 12 o'clock all traces of it had disappeared. It is warm enough at present to be without a fire. All are busy cooking up rations for fear we may have to leave. I haven't cut the ham you sent by Cullen, yet, and I have about half the middling which Mr. Christman brought me. I have one or two potatoes left yet. If we stay here until Spring, I think I shall have enough to last me. If you have an opportunity, I should like to have about a peck of peas. They go farther and do a man more good than anything that I know of.

I wish you would send my copy of Shakespeare; it's a brown colored back, with my name in it. Wrap it up and send it by May Warren, and ask him to give it to Pat Wooten; he promised to bring it for me. The needles you sent me are the very sizes I wanted. I am very much obliged to you for them. You need not send me any more paper and envelopes until I let you know, as I have five or six on hand and I want to use them up first. I have not received the letter yet that General Battle undertook to deliver for sister. His Brigade has been back for some week or more. Give my love to all the family, and believe me, as ever,

Your sincere and affectionate son,

WALTER.

Governor Vance [98]

Craig and Baker

CAMP NEAR ORANGE C. H., March 29, 1864.

My Dear Mother:

I wrote you a short letter only a few days ago, but as some little excitement outside of our regular routine of duty has occurred within the past few days, I thought I would drop you a little history of it. Governor Vance arrived among us last Friday evening, and was the guest of General Daniel.[99] He delivered a speech before that Brigade last Saturday evening. ALL the Generals of note in this army were present and on the stage with him, embracing Generals Lee, Ewell, A. P. Hill,[100] Stewart, Wilcox,[101] Rodes[102] and a good many others whose names I did not know; there were some twelve or fifteen in number. I did not hear but a part of the speech, as the crowd was so large that I could not get in a hundred yards of him.

Yesterday there was a grand review of all the North Carolina troops that is in this Corps, by Gov. Vance, including the cavalry. After the review the troops were all arranged around a stage erected for the purpose in the camp of the Thirtieth Regiment, and he addressed them with a speech of three or four hours length. He had the whole assembly in an uproar in less than two minutes after he arose. He said it did not sound right to him to address us as "Fellow Soldiers," because he was not one of us — he used to be until he shirked out of the service for a little office down in North Carolina, so now he would address us as "Fellow Tar Heels," as we always stick.

I was in a good place to hear every word that he said, and I don't think I ever listened to a more able speech of the kind in my life. It was very able and deep, interspersed with anecdotes, illustration of his subject, which kept the men from feeling fatigued. The review took up some two hours, marching all over the fields, and then we had to stand up all the while the speech was being delivered. Nearly the whole camp was there, in fact, there were thousands that could not hear him from their distance.

There was some dozen or two ladies present. After Gov. Vance got through, the crowd called for General Early.[103] He arose and spoke a short time, then General Rodes; after he was through Gov. Vance arose again and said he must talk a little more, too. He related two or three anecdotes relative to the Yankee characters and then retired amidst deafening "Rebel Yells." This morning it's cold and has just commenced raining. I think it will end in a snow. The last of the big snow has gone. Clarke's mountain is covered yet. I forgot to tell you that I received your letter night before last. My love to all.

Believe me, as ever, yours, etc.

WALTER.

Craig and Baker

My Dear Sister:[104]

Once more in our same old quarters, though we little thought a week ago that we would ever live to see them again. We had a very quiet time on picket this week, at the same time the most pleasant we have had this winter. Only one day and night of rain, the rest of the time the most delightful kind of weather. The boys when not on duty amused themselves at various sports, some fishing, some digging ground hogs out of their holes (an animal that I never saw until I came to Virginia), while nearly the whole regiment amused themselves gathering wild onions. The doctors recommend them very highly on account of their preventing scurvy. Gen. Ransom[105] had a kettle for each company brought down the line, for the purpose of cooking them. We had one man[106] from our regiment Company D to desert while on his post. He left his gun and accoutrements and swam the river.

Last Tuesday the Yankees had a tremendous cannonading going on for upwards of two hours. Just across the river we could hear the balls flying through the air and also hear them explode. The most reasonable supposition of the cause was that they were practicing previous to their attacking us. We have a rumor today that they have fallen back towards Centerville, whether it be true or not, there were plenty of them on the river this morning when we left. Col. Grimes took our band down with us this time, and every night they would get on a high bluff on the banks of the river and give the Yankees a serenade, closing with *Dixie* and the *Old North State*. Sometimes one of their bands would strike up in answer. The week before we went down, there was a Yankee Sergeant deserted and came over to us, reporting that Grant was to have attacked us last Sunday morning. The whole picket force were under arms that morning two hours before day ready to receive him. I was on the outpost that night and just before day, could not help from wishing that they would come across and attack our breastworks. But Sunday came and passed and everything remained quiet on both sides.

The man who told you we were suffering for bread was mistaken. Our meat is very slim, though we make out very well. As for bread we get more than we can eat. There is not a man in our company who has not got him a bag of extra meal, gradually increased from his daily rations. We draw just as much sugar and coffee as we could wish for. Meat is the only thing we are stinted with. We have not drawn any beef or ham in a month or two. We have (that is General Lee has) just received an official telegram from North Carolina stating that Gen. Hoke[107] had captured sixteen hundred prisoners and twenty-five pieces of cannon at Plymouth,[108] that's cheering news indeed, particularly from North Carolina. I hope Washington and Newbern may fall likewise. My love to all.

Your devoted brother,

WALTER.

Craig and Baker

A soldier of the Legion lay dying in Algiers,
There was lack of woman's nursing, there was dearth of
woman's tears;
But a comrade stood beside him, while his lifeblood ebbed away,
And bent, with pitying glances, to hear what he might say.
The dying soldier faltered, and he took that comrade's hand,
As he said, "I never more shall see my own, my native land;
Take a message, and a token, to some distant friends of mine,
For I was born at Bingen, — at Bingen on the Rhine."
His trembling voice grew faint and hoarse,
His grasp was childish, weak, —
His eyes put on a dying look, —
He sighed and ceased to speak.
His comrade bent to lift him,
But the spark of life had fled, —
The soldier of the Legion in a foreign land is dead!
And the soft moon rose up slowly,
And calmly she looked down
On the red sand of the battle-field,
With bloody corses strewn,
Yes, calmly on that dreadful scene
Her pale light seemed to shine,
As it shone on distant Bingen, — fair Bingen — on the Rhine.
— CAROLINE E. NORTON.

IN LINE OF BATTLE NEAR SPOTSYLVANIA
COURT HOUSE, VA., May 14, 1864.

My Dear Folks:

Through the kind providence of the Almighty God I have come out so far safe and sound and am spared once more to gladden your hearts by writing you. I scarcely know what to write you about or where to commence. Pen cannot describe or words relate the many adventures which we have passed through during the past ten days. We have been fighting to-day, makes eleven days and we have repulsed and whipped the Yankees every time they have attacked us. God only knows how much longer the battle will last, but if we are as successful in the future as we thus far have been, Grant may continue the battle for a month so far as I care. In that time I don't think he will have a single man left. His loss up to the present time is estimated at seventy thousand. Our loss is comparatively small, as we fought them most of the time in our breastworks. Last Sunday is the first time our brigade had any regular engagement with the enemy, though we had charged them several times and run them from their positions without firing a gun.

Last Sunday about 8 o'clock it was ascertained that the Yankees had made a flank movement and were making for Richmond by Spotsylvania Court House. We were almost worn out with fatigue from marching or loss of sleep when we started from this place to front them. I don't think I ever saw a hotter day in all my life. The men were fainting by the dozens, and very frequently one would drop dead in his tracks from overheat. The distance was about eighteen miles. We had gotten in about six miles of the place, when Gen. Ramseur rode down the line with a dispatch from Gen. Longstreet stating that he had repulsed the enemy with heavy loss, and that if the troops could hold out to get there in time to meet the second attack, in case the enemy made one, everything would be right.

Craig and Baker

He appealed to his brigade to know if they would go. The answer was a shout that we would. Some of the men were so tired and worn out they could hardly halloo. I was among that number, when in about three miles of this place I was forced to drop from overheat, and the brigade left me. I never hated anything so bad in all my life before, so much as to be left behind as then. The brigade had left about an hour when I heard the enemy's cannon open. It was like an electric shock to me, I bounced up and determined to go or die. I threw away everything I had but my gun and accoutrements, including three days' rations that I had not tasted since drawing them (without thinking where I was to get any more), and caught up with the brigade in about fifteen minutes before we charged the enemy and fought them until after dark. Our loss this night was small. The night was spent in building our breastworks.

Last Thursday though is the day that will be remembered by both armies as long as one man is left to tell the tale. At daylight they attacked the line a little to our right, drove our men out of both lines of breastworks and the result was hanging in the scales when our brigade was taken from one position and moved around in front of them. The stars and stripes were floating proudly all along our works when the order was given to "forward without firing." We commenced moving up pretty briskly, when our men commenced falling so fast, that the order was given to "double quick." No sooner said than done. We rushed forward with a yell and took the first line of works like a flash. We remained there long enough to fire a round or two and clear the way in front of us, when the order came to charge the other. We took that also with a large number of prisoners, then the fight commenced in earnest. It was a continuous charge and a war of musketry from that time, nine o'clock, until three o'clock in the morning, when we evacuated that line for another which had been established and fortified during the night. There is not a man in this brigade who will ever forget the sad requiem, which those minie balls sung over the dead and dying for twenty-two long hours; they put one in mind of some musical instrument; some sounded like wounded men crying; some like humming of bees; some like cats in the depth of the night, while others cut through the air with only a "Zip" like noise. I know it to be the hottest and the hardest fought battle that has even been on this continent. You would hardly recognize any of us at present. Every one looks as if he had passed through a hard spell of sickness, black and muddy as hogs. There was no one too nice that day to drop himself behind the breastworks. Brigadiers and Colonels lay as low in the trench and water as the men. It rained all that day and night, and the water was from three to six inches deep all along. If it had been winter the last man would have been frozen. I am too worn out to write anything of any interest. I am about half dead yet, as is every one else from the effects of the cannonading. My love to all, and believe me, your sincere son,

WALTER.

Craig and Baker

IN LINE BATTLE NEAR SPOTSYLVANIA COURT
HOUSE, VA., May 17, 1864.

My Dear Mother:

Again by kind Providence I am permitted to write you a short letter. There has been no general engagement since I last wrote you. Fights and skirmishing are kept up along the line. Our brigade is now the extreme left of the whole army. Cavalry joins us on our left. What Grant is waiting for it is impossible to say. It is rumored through camps that he has gone to Washington to consult with Lincoln. I do not think it is possible to have any harder fighting than we had last Thursday. Our brigade did some of the hardest fighting that day and night that has been done during the war. It is hard to realize what our brigade did actually accomplish that day. That morning at day break the enemy attacked Johnson's whole division and took their breastworks from them, together with fifteen or twenty pieces of artillery, which endangered the whole of Ewell's corps, owing to the nature of the position which he held. Our brigade, after we had charged and run the Yankees from their works, was not long enough to cover the line held by Johnston's division, so the Yankees held a position on our right, upon a hill which enabled them to keep up an incessant enfilading fire upon us; two thirds of the men which we lost were done in that way. Men were killed while squatting just as low and as close to the breastworks as it was possible for them to get. Tom Atkinson, poor fellow, was shot through the head, right by my side, another man in Company "E" was killed on the other; the man in front was shot through the body. I did not realize then what a hot place we were in. It was a wonder to me that the last one of us was not killed. We were exposed to that fire for twenty-two hours. Gen. Rodes sent word to Gen. Ramseur he would send his reinforcements, but Gen. R. sent him word that he had taken the position and he was confident his brigade would hold it. All he wanted to let us alone and send us ammunition, which he did. I shot away 120 rounds of cartridges myself, three cartridge boxes full.

Friday morning about an hour before day, we evacuated the works, which had been thrown up during the night by the entire pioneer force of the whole army. I don't suppose there is any man that can express the relief he felt after getting out of such a place. Our rations were out the evening before and we had orders to be ready to move next morning at 3 o'clock. We did not have time to fill our canteens, so we did not have a mouthful to eat or drink when we went into the fight. The ditches behind the works were from three to six inches deep in mud and water, and in addition to it it was raining incessantly from light that morning until we left the works the next morning after.

You can form some idea what our feelings would have been, putting all these privations together, had there been no danger attending, but add to all this the thought that the next minute may be your last, is another thing altogether. There is not a man in this brigade who will ever forget it. I forgot to mention in my last that Burton's leg was broken and he fell in the hands of the enemy. Pat Wooten was also wounded on the leg. Hoping that kind Providence may spare me to see the end of this great struggle, I remain, as ever, your sincere and affectionate son,

WALTER.

Craig and Baker

Dear Mother:

You will undoubtedly be surprised and I fear alarmed to receive a letter from me at this place. But do not let your mind feel
any uneasiness at all. Kind providence has so far favored me that
I have passed through another very severe battle with only a skin
wound on the inside of my knee. Though the exposure that we
had to endure that evening and night (Thursday, the 19th inst.),
was most too much for me. We fought for three or four hours in
the evening, in a drenching rain, until night coming on, we recti-
fied our lines, threw up some little breastworks with our bayonets, anticipating a night attack by the Yankees. Our lines were
in speaking distance of each other. The Yankees would give us a
cheer, then our boys would answer with a deafening Rebel Yell.
Gen. Ramseur hallooed out to them twice, "Come on Yankees,"
but they did not choose to do so, though I believe they tried to
make their men charge us, as we would hear their commands
to that effect. We lay there about half the night, in the mud and
water, behind our little mound of earth thrown up with our
bayonets and hands, when we were ordered to fall back as quietly
as possible.

Such a command at such a time puts a strange feeling on a
person, a relief to the mind which I can't describe, nor any one
realize, but those who have once been placed in that situation. I
always have had a horrible idea of a night attack, and I do hope
I may never have to encounter one. We marched back to our
breastworks that night (about six miles). Reached there about day
break; since then I have been troubled with weakness in the back
and a general exhaustion from over fatigue. I was not able to keep
up and do duty with the regiment, so I was sent off with a lot of
wounded, as that was no place for a sick man, looking for a big
fight at any moment. I think I shall be recruited enough in a week

or so to return. Don't feel any anxiety on my account, as everything may turn out for the best. Write me at this place as soon as
you receive this.

Yours, etc.,

WALTER.

P.S. Don't either of you get uneasy on my account and try to
come out here. I will let you know if I get bad off to need your
attention. I have written you two letters since the fighting commenced; did you receive them? Send me a sheet of paper as soon
as you receive this, and I will write you again immediately.

Craig and Baker

CAMP NEAR BUNKER HILL, VA., Aug. 30, 1864.

Dear Mother:

I take this occasion to drop you a few lines, as you will be more likely to get it if I send it by Capt. Thompson than by mail. I got with the regiment last Saturday at Bunker Hill, as they fell back from Charlestown.[109] We went into camp and remained quietly until yesterday morning when the Yankees advanced on Martinsburg pike. We were thrown in line of battle and remained so all day; the Yankees having retired we went back into camp a little after dark. We received orders last night to be ready to move this morning at sunrise. 'Tis now about eleven o'clock and we are still in camp and will probably remain here the remainder of the day, though two or three days is a long time for us to remain in camp without some move. The boys all seem to be in very good spirits, though they look quite thin from the hard marching they have had to do since they left Richmond. It's my opinion that the army will fall back towards Strasburg in a few days, though it's only a conjecture of my own. I have been in excellent health ever since I left home, though at times I have had the blues pretty bad. I begin to feel perfectly at home and everything begins to feel like old times. I am in hopes we have done most of our hard marching that is the only thing I am dreading now. The weather has turned some cooler, the nights are quite cool, making a heavy blanket feel quite comfortable.

Tell Mr. Rhodes that Blake is with the Company and is looking very well, he was only at the hospital a few days from being broken down. He is asleep now, or I would ask him if he wished to send any message. Write soon. My love to all the family. I remain as ever,

Your sincere and affectionate son,

WALTER.

UNITED STATES PRISONERS CAMP,
POINT LOOKOUT, MD., Sept. 29, 1864.

My Dear Mother:

At the battle of Winchester, fought the 19th of this month, myself, together with seven others of our company, were captured, namely Henry Warren, Emerson Winstead, Pat Wooten, Bunyan Barnes,[110] Edwin Barnes,[111] Byrant Stokes[112] and Joel Taylor.[113] All of us are in very good health. All of us have written although some of our letters may be lost. Give my love to all the family. Please write as soon as you receive this. Direct me care of Major Brady,[114] Provost Marshal. Let me know whether Blake was killed or wounded. Goodbye, believe me as ever.

Your sincere and affectionate son,

WALTER.

When I remember all
　　The friends, so linked together,
I've seen around me fall,
Like leaves in wintry weather,
I feel like one
Who treads alone
Some banquet hall deserted,
Whose light are fled,
Whose garlands dead,
And all but he departed;
Thus, in the stilly night,
Ere slumber's chain has bound me,
Sad memory brings the light
Of other days around me.
　　— THOMAS MOORE.

Craig and Baker

CAMP THREE MILES NORTH OF PETERSBURG,
Christmas Day, Dec. 25, 1864.

My Dear Mother:

I intended to have written the day after getting here, but it
rained all day and the coldest kind of a rain too. The next day we
received orders to move. We had almost completed our winter
quarters and the boys hated to leave very much. We did not think
at the time we should ever come back again, though some men
from each company was left in camp to take care of the things. I
was the one from our company left.

Last Thursday about sunset the division left and camped
in a mile or two of Drury's Bluff,[115] some ten miles from here.
Last night about 9 o'clock they returned. We shall complete our
quarters in two or three days now. To-day being Sunday and
Xmas too, the boys think we should rest. It is the gloomiest Xmas
that I ever saw. We not only miss the extras which we have had
heretofore, but we have not got as much meat or bread as we
can eat. The Xmas dinner promised to Lee's army, I see in the
papers, has been postponed until New Year's day. I doubt then
whether we get any as we are not in the entrenchments, though
I think we deserve it as much as they do. We have done as much
hard fighting and as for the marching we have done all. The boys
were all very glad to see us. Gen. Grimes happened to ride by as I
arrived and was pulling my things off. He stopped and had quite
a long chat, he seemed right glad to see me back. Col. Venable,[116]
one of Gen. Lee's staff, told Gen. Grimes, who is in command
of the division now, to make his men as comfortable as possible,
that we would in all probability remain here all the winter, unless
something turned up unforeseen at present. I am in hopes it may
be so, for I think our division needs rest if any troops in the army
do. I understand we came here to relieve some of the troops
in the fortification, but as they had made themselves comfortable, they would not be relieved. They preferred to remain in the

works on the front line. I think they are sensible too, for I expect they will have us running all around, just as we did the past two or three days, all winter. I almost wish we had been sent South instead of Hoke's division. In passing through Raleigh I stayed all night at the "Way-Side-Inn."[117] Next morning in rolling up my blankets I forgot to put my socks in and came off and left them. I never hated anything so bad in my life. Just think they were the only extra pieces of clothing I took along, and then should lose them. If McBride[118] has not left before you receive this please send me another pair. If you have any extra butter at the time just wrap a rag around a small ball and get him to bring that along. It is the best way to send it in cold weather. He will have to walk about a mile from where the cars stop to our camp. The cars stop two miles this side of Petersburg, for fear of being shelled. Blake has gone to Petersburg today on a pass. He is looking very well. I called to see Uncle Richard[119] while in Raleigh, the only relative I saw. Raleigh has sadly changed in four years. Give my love to all the family.

Your affectionate son,

WALTER.

General Robert E. Lee

CAMP FOURTH NORTH CAROLINA REGIMENT,
COX'S BRIGADE, RODES' DIVISION,
NEAR PETERSBURG, VA.,
January 15, 1865.

My Dear Mother:

McBride came night before last and brought everything safely, except the butter. He looked all over his baggage and we searched the box thoroughly, but could not find it. The articles which you sent me were the very articles which we needed most, especially the peas. We draw one third of a pound of meat now and we make out very well. You need not send me any more meat, as you need that more than we do. Send such things as peas, potatoes and such things as you make plenty of and do not have to buy. We are very comfortably fixed up in our winter quarters now. We have been busy cleaning up for the past two weeks and I shall be glad when we finish. The boys have gone into these quarters with less spirit than any we have ever built. We would not be surprised at any moment to receive marching orders, and none of us have any idea of staying here until spring. The greater part of the soldiers seem to be in low spirits and a good many say the Confederacy has "gone up" (as they term it), and that we are whipped. I have never seen the men so discouraged before. I hear also that the men are deserting the front lines and going home by large squads. If this is true and it is continued long, the Yankees will whip us certain. It is the opinion here that Richmond is to be evacuated this winter. That has a very demoralizing effect on the men also. I hardly think that General Lee will risk a battle around Richmond in the spring, unless he gets more men. I don't think there will be any general engagement here during the winter. The sharpshooters keep everything alive on the lines day and night. Every dark and cloudy night they keep up such a heavy fire as to resemble a line of battle; although we are some four miles off, we hear every musket that is fired, as distinctly as if it was fired in our own camp. Every two or three days the batteries on each side take a notion to have a little duel, and for an hour or two there is a cannon shot for nearly every minute, then gradually dies out. It used to make me feel a little uneasy at first, for when we were in the valley and heard a cannon every man would fix up his things, and by the time he got that done, marching orders would come, but here we do not mind it any more than if nothing was going on. The box of blankets which we sent to Richmond last winter, and the one in which my shawl was packed, came the other day. Lieut. Wells expects to go home in a few days and I shall send it home by him. I drew a new blanket and also a pair of good woolen socks which, with the ones you sent me by Mac, will last me the rest of the winter.

Give my love to all.

Your affectionate son,

WALTER.

CAMP FOURTH NORTH CAROLINA REGIMENT, NEAR PETERSBURG, January 18, 1865.

Dear Sister:

I send by the boy Church,[120] a pair of shoes and a pair of socks. Brother can have the shoes fixed up and wear them. I guess they will fit him. I never expect to wear them again. The socks only need a little darning to make them serviceable. I shall let you know when I shall need any more. The book I send is a pretty story of the present war. Everything seems to be unusually quiet. I understand picket firing has been stopped on the lines. We haven't heard any for several days, neither have we heard any cannonading. The peace question is all the excitement in camp now. From what I saw in the "Examiner" this morning I think myself there is something in the wind. I do hope peace will be made before spring. The men are getting very discouraged, and to tell the truth, they have cause to be. Some of our regiment was down on the lines Sunday, and they say the troops have not had any meat for five days. If the men are not fed they will not stay with the army. They are deserting from the lines every night, and going to the Yankees. Don't send me anything else that you will have to buy, or need before the end of the year. We expect to go on picket this coming Sunday, to be gone a week. My love to all.

Your devoted brother,

WALTER.

CAMP FOURTH NORTH CAROLINA REGIMENT,
NEAR PETERSBURG, VA., Jan. 29, 1865.

My Dear Folks:

I received your letter dated 20th inst., yesterday, which made nine days that it has been on the way.

Last week we spent on the front lines doing picket duty in the place of Scales Brigade which has been sent off. We had an awful time; the whole week it rained, and sleeted part of the time, and the rest of the time, it kept up the coldest wind that I ever felt. The men on vidette[121] had to be relieved every half hour, to keep from freezing. One man in our regiment got so cold he could hardly talk when he was relieved. On the right of our brigade, the Yankees were some six or eight hundred yards off, but on the left we were near enough to talk to each other in an ordinary tone of voice, though we were not allowed to speak to them or to communicate with them in any way. We had two men to desert our regiment and go to the enemy. They were two brothers. I am afraid we will have more desertions in the spring than we have ever had yet. The men are getting very must dissatisfied. The Consolidation Bill, which is to be carried into effect shortly will cause a good deal of desertion among our best soldiers. I am afraid our company and regiment will lose their name after all the hard service which we have done since the commencement of the war. There are a good many peace rumors circulating through camp, which gives the men something to talk about. I fear it will all end in another summer's hard fighting. If Blake comes by home, when he starts back, you may send me a gallon of peas and some potatoes. You need not send anything that you will have to buy. I expect we draw as much meat here in the army as you can afford to eat at home. I hope something will turn up by spring which will enable me to go home. I should like very much to see a good crop growing on our little places. What does brother[122] intend doing in case the war continues? I hope he will never have to go. If he does, anything is preferable to infantry in the field.

Give my love to all.

Yours affectionately,

WALTER.

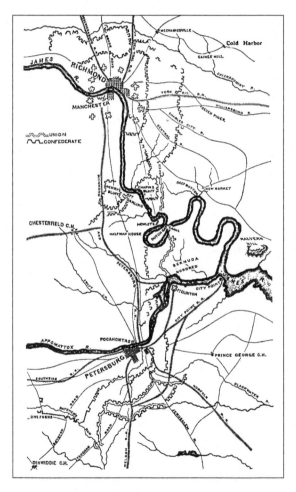

Richmond and Petersburg

CAMP. COX'S BRIGADE, NEAR PETERSBURG, VA.,
February 14, 1865.

My Dear Mother:

I would have written on receipt of your letter and box, which
you sent me, but the troops were off at the time and there was
no means of mailing a letter. Our division was ordered down on
the extreme right last Sunday a week ago, to meet the Yankees at
Hatcher's Run.[123] Our division was not engaged; the other two
divisions of our corps did some fighting before we got there.
The troops were gone about a week, and they suffered consider-
ably from the cold. It was snowing and sleeting when they left. I
missed the pleasure of that trip. I have been permanently detailed
at brigade headquarters in charge of a guard, to guard quartermaster's stores, and things generally among the wagon yards. I
have three in charge, and all I have to do is to see that they do
their duty. We have our quarters separate, and nothing to do
but keep up one post at night. We have no other duty whatever
to do, not even to answer to roll call. Capt. Jones,[124] our A. A.
General, who gave me the detail, told me to select my own men,
so I took one from our company, so that I might have an agree-
able bedfellow and messmate. George Winstead[125] is his name.
Wiley Winstead's brother. I am just as comfortably fixed now as I
could wish to be out here. I shall miss all the trips the troops will
have to make during the winter, such as picket duty, and all raids
to head off the "Yankees" unless we break up this camp entirely.
Our brigade goes on picket this morning, Saturday. I am very
much obliged to you for the box of provisions.

I expect there is a movement on hand now, as there is an
order to issue three days' rations to the men. Marching orders do
not trouble me so much now, as the guard is always apt to guard
the forage, etc., which is left in camp. I think of home every time
I take out my little ball of butter to eat with a roasted potato at
night before bed time. George Winstead got a few potatoes from

Craig and Baker

home the same day my box came. I generally spend most of my time reading whatever I am able to borrow. I wish I could get something that would be more useful to me than novels. I hope Blake got my shawl home all safe. Give my love to all the family. Dossey has just been in to see me on his way back to camp. He has been to Petersburg on business for Gaston.[126] He is very well.

Your sincere and affectionate son,

WALTER.

WAGON YARD, COX'S BRIGADE, NEAR
PETERSBURG, VA., March 23rd, 1865.

My Dear Mother:

I received your letter, bearing the date of March 14th, a few minutes ago. It seems that about nine days is the average length of time for a letter to come from home here. I wrote you a letter just before we left the old camp, which you have doubtless received ere this. We have moved twice since I wrote that letter. After the first move, we were temporarily attached to Mahone's Division, the last move we made we joined our own division, which is in the entrenchments in front of Petersburg. Our Brigade is on the extreme left of it, between the Appomattox River and Swift Creek, with the river between us and the Yankees.

I have not been down on the lines since we last moved, but I hear that it is a very good place, inasmuch as we will hardly be attacked in our front as long as we stay there. I am still staying with Capt. Faircloth[127] in the Q. M. Department, but when the campaign opens, I expect to go back to the company, as every man that can handle a gun will be needed there. Richmond and Petersburg have not been evacuated yet, tho' there is still rumors that the latter place will be. The papers are not allowed to publish any war news, so we are as completely ignorant as you are as to what is going on. I am very uneasy for fear that Sherman's[128] army will not be checked before we have to evacuate Richmond and Peterburg. If that army could only be whipped, and it must be, or we can't stay in Virginia, I would still feel confident of the final results. There are a good many of our soldiers deserting to the enemy, but I am in hopes we will have enough left to keep the Yankees in check on this line. I feel a good deal of anxiety on account of Cullen's having to go in service so soon. I would not have him join this regiment for anything. If he cannot obtain a better place, I will try and get him into Manley's Battery[129] from Raleigh, which, if he does have to go into active service right

Craig and Baker

away, will be the best place that I can think of. It is on the lines, some two miles to our left, where it has been about ten months, without losing a man in battle. If he was in that company, he would see a much easier time than he would in Infantry, being small, he would be very apt to be made a driver and in time of fights hold the horses in the rear, or in some place where they can be sheltered. What time will he be seventeen? Write to me as soon as you receive this, and let me know what he thinks about it. In the meantime, I will go over to Manley's Battery and see if I can get him in. I fear that it will be full, as I know a good many young men who joined on coming seventeen. It is a very good company and composed of a great many very nice men. I knew some of them before the war. I am intimately acquainted with all of the officers. Baz. Manley is Capt. Bunny Guion,[130] James Powell[131] and James McKimmon,[132] the Lieutenant, all from Raleigh. Tell Cullen to take my advice and never join this Regiment as long as he can avoid it. However much I would like to have him with me. I am giving him this advice for his own good. Please think about the matter and write me immediately. Give my love to all the family. Where is sister? Is she at Wilson? I will write again in a few days, probably before I hear from you. Tell Cullen to write when you do. Goodbye.

Your affectionate son,

WALTER

As You May
Never See
Us Again

... they have passed

Craig and Baker

*A*las, *these letters are all that is left of the two noble sons and brothers, for George was killed at the battle of Seven Pines while Walter died from exposure after that terrible battle he so vividly describes in one of his letters. "Requiescat in pace" to all who fell in those days in that cruel war.*

"All quiet along the Potomac," they say,
Except now and then a stray picket
Is shot as he walks on his beat, to and fro,
By a rifleman hid in the thicket;
'Tis nothing, a private or two, now and then,
Will not count in the news of the battle,
Not as officers lost — only one of the men
Moaning out, all alone the death rattle."
— ETHEL LYNN BEERS

Company F, 4th North Carolina Infantry
Source: *Roster of North Carolina Troops 1861-1865*

ALLISON, James
Mustered in 1/1/64 as Private. Previous service in Co. H, 40th N.C. Infantry.
Killed on 6/3/64.

ARMSTRONG, George Washington
20 years old, a resident of Wilson County, NC. Enlisted 6/28/61 at Craven
County, NC as a Private. Discharged 9/24/62 due to promotion as 2nd Lieutenant, Co. G, 5th NC Infantry.

ARQUIR, L. D.
Mustered in 4/18/61 as Private.

ATKINSON, Alvin
33 years old, a resident of Wilson County, NC. Enlisted 2/12/62 at Wilson
County, NC as a Private. Died of disease 5/24/62.

ATKINSON, James T.
24 years old, a resident of Wilson County, NC. Enlisted 6/28/61 at Craven
County, NC as a Private. Promoted Corporal 3/14/63. Promoted Sergeant
5/19/63. Captured at Fredricksburg, VA on 5/3/63, held as prisoner at Washington, DC. Exchanged at City Point, VA on 5/10/63. Killed at Spotsylvania
Court House, VA on 5/12/64.

ATKINSON, Jonas J.
24 years old, a resident of Wilson County, NC. Enlisted 6/28/61 at Craven
County, NC as a Private. Died of disease on 1/30/62 at Manassas, VA.

BAKER, Benjamin R.
22 years old, a resident of Wilson County, NC. Enlisted 6/28/61 at Craven
County, NC as a Private. Killed on 5/3/63 at Chancellorsville, VA.

BARNES, Bunyan
24 years old, a resident of Wilson County, NC. Enlisted 6/28/61 at Craven
County, NC as a Private. Wounded 6/5/62 (place not stated). Wounded
5/3/63 at Chancellorsville, VA. Returned to ranks 9/1/63. Captured 9/19/64
at Winchester, VA. Confined at Point Lookout, MD. Took Oath of Allegiance
on 6/3/65 at Point Lookout, MD.

BARNES, Edwin
33 years old, a resident of Wilson County, NC. Enlisted 2/12/62 at Wilson County, NC as a Private. Detailed as a teamster from 7/28/62 through 8/15/64. Captured 9/19/64 at Winchester, VA. Confined at Point Lookout, MD.

BARNES, Hardy H.
25 years old, a resident of Wilson County, NC. Enlisted 9/9/61 at Manassas, VA as a Private. Promoted Corporal on 1/1/63. Promoted Sergeant on 3/14/63. Wounded 5/3/63 at Chancellorsville, VA. Died of wounds 5/7/63.

BARNES, Jacob
28 years old, a resident of Wilson County, NC. Enlisted 6/28/61 at Craven County, NC as a Private. Killed 5/31/62 at Seven Pines, VA.

BARNES, Jesse S.
23 years old, a resident of Wilson County, NC. Enlisted 5/16/61 at Wilson County, NC as a Captain. Killed 5/31/62 at Seven Pines, VA.

BARNES, Lafayette
21 years old, a resident of Wilson County, NC. Enlisted 6/28/61 at Craven County, NC as a Private. Promoted 1st Sergeant. Died of typhoid fever at Plains Station, VA on 10/22/61.

BARNES, William B.
19 years old, a resident of Wilson County, NC. Enlisted 9/9/61 at Wilson County, NC as a Private. Died of wounds 6/11/64 at Lynchburg, VA.

BARNES, William S.
18 years old, a resident of Wilson County, NC. Enlisted 6/28/61 at Craven County, NC as a Corporal. Promoted Sergeant on 11/30/61. Promoted 1st Lieutenant and Adjutant on 3/14/63. Transferred to staff of Gen. Grimes on 6/14/64.

BATTLE, George W.
18 years old, residence Wilson County, NC, occupation a student. Enlisted 6/28/61 at Craven County, NC as Private. Died of wounds 6/6/62 at Richmond, VA.

BATTLE, Walter R.
21 years old a resident of Wilson County, NC. Enlisted 6/28/61 at Craven County, NC as Private. Wounded (date & place not stated), hospitalized 5/25/64 at Richmond, Va.(returned to duty). Captured on 9/19/64 at Winchester, VA. Confined 9/22/64 at Point Lookout. MD. Exchanged 11/15/64 at Venus Point, GA. Captured on 4/7/65 at Sutherland's Station, VA. Confined 4/10/65 at Point Lookout, MD. Released after taking Oath of Allegiance 6/23/65 at Point Lookout, MD.

BEACH, John R.
21 years old a resident of Wilson County, NC. Enlisted 6/28/61 at Craven County, NC as Private. Died of chronic diarrhea at Lynchburg, VA on 1/11/63

BEAMON, Joseph B.
27 years old a resident of Wilson County, NC. Enlisted 6/28/61 at Craven County, NC as Private. Died of variola confluent at Richmond, VA on 1/9/64.

BENTON, John L.
27 years old a resident of Wilson County, NC. Enlisted 6/28/61 at Craven County, NC as Private. Wounded on 5/31/62 at Seven Pines, VA. Died of wounds on 6/10/62.

BERNARD, Joseph B.
Enlisted on 6/23/63 at Wake County, NC as Private.

BILLINGER, W. M.
Enlisted as Private. Paroled on 4/21/65 at Farmville, VA.

BOWDEN, Whitford B.
A resident of Wilson County, NC. Enlisted 6/28/61 at Craven County, NC as Private. Discharged for being a minor on 10/19/61.

BRIDGERS, Edwin C.
19 years old a resident of Wilson County, NC. Enlisted 6/28/61 at Craven County, NC as Private. Killed on 9/16/61 at Manassas, VA.

BROWN, A. J.
Enlisted as Private. Paroled 5/11/65 at Greensboro, NC.

BURTON, John L.
19 years old a resident of Wilson County, NC. Enlisted 6/28/61 at Craven County, NC as Private.
Captured and paroled 9/27/62. Promoted Corporal on 5/7/63. Captured on 5/3/63 at Fredricksburg, VA. Paroled on 5/10/63 at City Point, VA. Wounded 5/15/64 at Old Wilderness Tavern, VA. Died of wounds on 6/16/64 at Fredricksburg, VA.

CHRISTMAN, Daniel P.
22 years old a resident of Wilson County, NC. Enlisted 6/28/61 at Craven County, NC as Private. Promoted Corporal on 1/22/63. Promoted Sergeant on 5/7/63. Surrendered at Appomattox Court House, VA on 4/9/65. Paroled on 5/13/65 at Greensboro, NC.

CLARK, Sidney P.
18 years old a resident of Wilson County, NC. Enlisted 6/28/61 at Craven County, NC as Private. Wounded and captured on 5/5/62 at Williamsburg, VA. Hospitalized 5/10/62 at Ft. Monroe, VA. Transferred on 7/15/62 to Ft. Delaware, DE. Exchanged on 8/5/62 at Aikenís Landing, VA. Commissioned 1st Lieutenant and transferred to Co. H, 59 NC Infantry on 9/24/62. Commissioned 1st Lieutenant in Company H, 4th North Carolina Cavalry on 1/2/63. Released and returned to regiment. Captured on 6/19/63 at Middleburg, VA. Confined on 6/22/63 at Old Capitol Prison, Washington, DC. Promoted Captain on 6/8/64. Transferred to Johnsonís Island, OH on 8/8/63. Transferred on 2/20/65 to Point Lookout, MD. Paroled on 5/1/65 at Goldsboro, NC.

COE, Wesley A.
Enlisted as Private. Paroled 5/8/65 at Greensboro, NC.

CONDON, Redmond
22 years old a resident of Wilson County, NC. Enlisted 6/28/61 at Craven County, NC as Private.
Wounded on 5/3/63 at Chancellorsville, VA. Detailed as a nurse 9/1/63 till 8/15/64.

COX, Lewis
25 years old a resident of Wilson County, NC. Enlisted 6/28/61 at Craven County, NC as Private. Discharged for disability on 1/7/63.

CRAFTON, Robert W.
18 years old a resident of Wilson County, NC. Enlisted 2/24/62 at Wilson County, NC as Private. Killed on 5/31/62 at Seven Pines, VA.

CROCKER, William A.
20 years old a resident of Wilson County, NC. Enlisted 2/12/62 at Wilson County, NC as Private. Reported sick on 5/31/62. Returned to regiment on 4/2/63. Deserted on 5/1/63 and returned to regiment. Hospitalized on 7/5/64 at Danville, VA. Deserted on 8/1/64 and returned to regiment. Paroled on 5/3/65 at Goldsboro, NC.

DAVIS, George C.
25 years old, born in Campbell County, VA, a resident of Wilson County, NC. Enlisted 6/28/61 at Craven County, NC as Private. Discharged for disability on 12/16/62 at Richmond, VA.

DAVIS, Joseph
34 years old a resident of Wilson County, NC. Enlisted 10/9/61 at Manassas, VA as a Private. Captured on 9/17/62 at Sharpsburg, MD. Exchanged on 3/12/63. Paroled on 5/15/65 at Goldsboro, NC.

DRIVER, Neverson A.
19 years old, born in Nash County, NC, a resident of Wilson County, NC. Enlisted 6/28/61 at Craven County, NC as Private. Discharged for disability on 3/20/63 at Hamiltonís Crossing, VA.

DRIVER, William A.
24 years old, a resident of Wilson County, NC. Enlisted on 7/30/61at Wilson County, NC as a Private. Mustered in on 8/30/61 into Co. E, 19 NC Infantry. Transferred to Co.F, 4th North Carolina Infantry on 4/4/63.

DUNHAM, John W.
18 years old, a resident of Wilson, NC. Enlisted 5/16/61 at Wilson County, NC as a 1st Lieutenant. Promoted Captain on 5/31/62. Wounded on 5/31/62 at Seven Pines, VA. Resigned due to wounds on 3/9/63.

EVANS, Arthur
31 years old, a resident of Wilson, NC. . Enlisted 4/18/62 at Wilson County, NC as a Private. Killed on 7/18/64 at Snickerís Gap, VA.

FARMER, James C.
19 years old, a resident of Wilson County, NC. Enlisted 6/28/61 at Craven County, NC as Private. Wounded on 5/31/62 at Seven Pines, VA. Transferred to Veteran Reserve Corps on 5/10/64.

FARMER, John B.
18 years old, a resident of Wilson County, NC. Enlisted 6/28/61 at Craven County, NC as Private. Promoted Corporal on 5/19/63. Killed at Spotsylvania Court House, VA on 5/10/64.

FARMER, Jonathan D.
19 years old, occupation a farmer, a resident of Wilson County, NC. Enlisted 5/15/62 at Wilson County, NC as Private. Wounded on 5/31/62 at Seven Pines, VA. Discharged on 7/5/62 at Richmond, VA. Died from wounds on 8/21/64.

FARMER, M.
A resident of Wilson County, NC. Paroled on 5/15/65 at Goldsboro, NC.

FARMER, Thaddeus M.
18 years old, a resident of Wilson County, NC. Enlisted on 5/15/62 at Wilson County, NC as a Private. Died on 6/30/62.

FARMER, Wiley
18 years old, a resident of Wilson County, NC. Enlisted on 7/5/61 at Wilson County, NC as a Private. Wounded on 5/31/62 at Seven Pines, VA. Detailed as hospital nurse from 3/28/63 till 8/15/64. Transferred to Veteran Reserve Corps on 1/2/65.

FARMER, William J.
18 years old, a resident of Wilson County, NC. Enlisted 6/28/61 at Craven County, NC as Private. Died of pneumonia on 10/11/61 at Plains Station, VA.

FARRELL, Gray
23 years old, a resident of Wilson County, NC. Enlisted 6/28/61 at Craven County, NC as Private. Died of typhoid on 10/11/61 at Plains Station, VA.

FELTON, Elisha
20 years old, a resident of Wilson County, NC. Enlisted 6/28/61 at Craven County, NC as Private.

FITZGERALD, C. W.
18 years old, a resident of Wilson County, NC. Enlisted 2/20/62 at Wilson County, NC as Private. Transferred on 12/28/63 to Pegram's Light Artillery.

FITZGERALD, William
24 years old, born in Cumberland County, NC, a resident of Wilson County, NC. Enlisted 6/28/61 at Craven County, NC as Private. Wounded 6/27/62 at Gaine's Mill, VA. Absent on 1/20/63. Wounded on 5/3/63 at Chancellorsville, VA. Died of wounds on 5/19/63.

FLORA, Elvin
A resident of Wilson County, NC. Enlisted 1/15/62 at Manassas, VA as a Private. Captured 9/17/62 at Sharpsburg, MD. Confined at Ft. Delaware, DE on 9/22/62. Exchanged on 11/10/62 at Aiken's Landing, VA. Captured on 5/3/63 at Fredricksburg, VA. Exchanged on 5/10/63 at City Point, VA. Wounded on 5/9/64 at Spotsylvania Court House, VA. Returned to regiment on 8/15/64. Hospitalized on 3/25/65 at Richmond, VA.

FRANKLIN, Rufus M.
25 years old, a resident of Wilson County, NC. Enlisted 6/28/61 at Craven County, NC as Private. Killed on 5/31/62 at Seven Pines, VA.

GARDNER, Theophilus
35 years old, a resident of Wilson County, NC. Enlisted 7/28/63 at Wake County, NC as Private. Detailed as Provost Guard from 11/24/63 through 10/15/64.

GAY, James
21 years old, a resident of Wilson County, NC. Enlisted 6/28/61 at Craven County, NC as Private. Promoted Corporal on 3/14/63. Wounded at Chancellorsville, VA on 5/3/63. Returned to regiment on 9/1/63. Promoted Sergeant on 9/30/63. Surrendered at Appomattox Court House, VA on 4/9/65.

HANSELL, William R.
27 years old, a resident of Wilson County, NC. Enlisted 6/28/61 at Craven County, NC as a Sergeant. Promoted 1st Sergeant. Transferred to Co. D, 44 North Carolina on 9/4/63.

HARRIS, David B.
18 years old, a resident of Wilson County, NC. Enlisted 6/28/61 at Craven County, NC as Private. Died of typhoid fever at Plains Station, VA on 10/27/61.

HARRISON, Edmund F.
38 years old, a resident of Wilson County, NC. Enlisted 6/28/61 at Craven County, NC as a Musician.

HEARN, William A.
19 years old, a resident of Wilson County, NC. Enlisted 6/28/61 at Craven County, NC as Private. Discharged on 2/13/62 at Manassas, VA.

HENDERSON, Robert
22 years old, occupation a miner, enlisted as a Private. Took Oath of Allegiance on 4/9/65.

HOWARD, P.
Residence Wilson County, NC. Enlisted as a Private. Paroled at Goldsboro, NC.

JACKSON, Doctor G.
20 years old, a resident of Wilson County, NC. Enlisted 6/28/61 at Craven County, NC as Private. Captured 9/17/62 at Sharpsburg, MD, confined at Ft. Delaware, DE. Exchanged 11/10/62 at Aikenís Landing, VA. Wounded on 5/3/63 at Chancellorsville, VA. Captured and confined in Old Capital Prison, Washington, DC. Exchanged at City Point, VA on 6/30/63. Returned to regiment on 9/1/63. Paroled on 4/24/65.

JACKSON, George W.
18 years old, a resident of Wilson County, NC. Enlisted 6/28/61 at Craven County, NC as Private. Promoted to Musician on 2/11/63.

JACKSON, Henry L.
28 years old, a resident of Wilson County, NC. Enlisted 4/1/62 at Pitt County, NC as Private. Killed on 5/19/64 at Spotsylvania Court House.

KNIGHT, Thomas D.
18 years old, a resident of Wilson County, NC. Enlisted 6/28/61 at Craven County, NC as Private. Wounded on 5/3/63 at Chancellorsville, VA. A Pris-

Craig and Baker

oner of War on 5/13/63. Returned to regiment on 9/1/63. Absent from ranks on 5/2/64. Hospitalized on 9/17/64 at Richmond, VA. Returned to regiment on 11/10/64. Captured 4/3/65 at Petersburg, VA. Took Oath of Allegiance at Hartís Island, NY on 6/17/65.

LANCASTER, Benjamin H.
34 years old, a resident of Wilson County, NC. Enlisted 6/28/61 at Craven County, NC as Private. Surrendered on 4/9/65 at Appomatox Court House.

LANCASTER, Robert R
26 years old, a resident of Wilson County, NC. Enlisted 6/28/61 at Craven County, NC as Sergeant. Wounded in action. Died on 1/22/63 of typhoid fever at Wilson County, NC.

LANCASTER, William E.
18 years old, a resident of Wilson County, NC. Enlisted 6/28/61 at Craven County, NC as Private. Captured 9/17/62 at Sharpsburg, MD. Confined at Ft. Delaware, DE. Exchanged on 11/10/62 at Aikenís Landing, VA. Died on 1/15/63.

LANGLEY, Van B. W.
23 years old, a resident of Wilson County, NC. Enlisted 6/28/61 at Craven County, NC as Private. Died of typhoid fever on 11/4/61 at Manassas, VA.

LEE, Thomas G.
22 years old, a resident of Wilson County, NC. Enlisted 6/28/61 at Craven County, NC as a Corporal. Reduced to Private on 9/30/61. Promoted 1st Sergeant of Company E on 11/1/62. Promoted Captain on 3/18/63. Wounded on 5/3/63 at Chancellorsville, VA. Promoted 2nd Lieutenant of Company D on 8/3/63. Hospitalized for wounds on 5/15/64 at Richmond, VA. Surrendered on 4/9/65 at Appomattox Court House, VA.

LEWIS, William H.
23 years old, a resident of Wilson County, NC. Enlisted 6/28/61 at Craven County, NC as a Private. Died of typhoid fever and pneumonia on 11/5/61 at Manassas, VA.

LEWIS, William T.
25 years old, a resident of Wilson County, NC. Enlisted 6/28/61 at Craven County, NC as a Private. Promoted Corporal. Killed on 5/31/62 at Seven Pines, VA.

MARTIN, R. J.
Enlisted as a 2nd Lieutenant. Captured on 9/22/64 at Fisherís Hill, VA. Confined on 9/25/64 at Old Capitol Prison, Washington, DC. Transferred to Ft. Delaware, DE on 2/4/65.

McBRIDE, John
32 years old, a resident of Wilson County, NC. Enlisted 6/28/61 at Craven County, NC as a Private. Promoted Commissary Sergeant on 4/9/62. Reduced to Sergeant on 9/30/63. Surrendered on 4/9/65 at Appomatox Court House, VA.

McDONALD, Thomas
Enlisted as a Private. Captured on 7/15/64 at Harperís Ferry, WV. Confined on 7/20/64 at Washington, DC.

MARLOW, Pheasanton B.
23 years old, a resident of Wilson County, NC. Enlisted 6/28/61 at Craven County, NC as a Private. Wounded on 5/31/62 at Seven Pines, VA. Transferred on 6/12/64 to Veteran Reserve Corps

MARLOW, William D.
19 years old, a resident of Wilson County, NC. Enlisted 6/28/61 at Craven County, NC as a Private. Killed on 5/31/62 at Seven Pines, VA.

MARSHBOURN, Samuel D.
18 years old, a resident of Wilson County, NC. Enlisted 6/28/61 at Craven County, NC as a Private. Assigned to Pioneer Corps from 6/27/62 through 8/15/64.

MARSHBOURNE, James H.
19 years old, a resident of Wilson County, NC. Enlisted 6/28/61 at Craven County, NC as a Private. Promoted Corporal on 3/13/63. Wounded and captured on 5/3/63 at Fredricksburg, VA. Confined in Washington, DC. Exchanged on 5/10/63 at Snickerís Gap, VA. Returned to regiment on 9/1/63. Promoted Sergeant on 9/10/63. Wounded on 7/18/64. Captured on 4/6/65 at Burkeville, VA. Confined at Newport News, VA. Took Oath of Allegiance on 6/30/65 at Newport News, VA.

MEEKS, William L.
20 years old, a resident of Wilson County, NC. Enlisted 6/28/61 at Craven County, NC as a Private. Killed on 5/31/62 at Seven Pines, VA.

MINOR, John H.
21 years old, a resident of Wilson County, NC. Enlisted 6/28/61 at Craven County, NC as a Private. Killed on 5/31/62 at Seven Pines, VA.

MINSHEW, John H.
28 years old, occupation a merchant, a resident of Wilson County, NC. Enlisted 6/28/61 at Craven County, NC as a Private. Hospitalized on 2/21/63 at Ruchmond, VA. Died of pneumonia on 4/1/63.

MIXON, Langely
22 years old, a resident of Wilson County, NC. Enlisted 6/28/61 at Craven County, NC as a Private. Wounded and captured on 5/3/63 at Fredricksburg, VA. Confined at Old Capital Prison, Washington, DC. Exchanged on 6/25/63 at City Point, VA. Returned to regiment on 9/1/63. Transferred to Confederate Navy on 4/5/64.

MORE, W.J.
Enlisted as a Private. Paroled on 5/6/65 at Greensboro, NC.

MOYE, Lemuel H.
33 years old, a resident of Wilson County, NC. Enlisted 6/28/61 at Craven County, NC as a Private. Died of pneumonia on 12/2/62 at Gordonsville, VA.

NOLLY, William B.
18 years old, occupation a farmer, a resident of Wilson County, NC. Enlisted 6/28/61 at Craven County, NC as a Private. Killed on 7/1/63 at Gettysburg, PA.

OETTINGER, Leopold
21 years old, a resident of Wilson County, NC. Enlisted 6/28/61 at Craven County, NC as a Private. Killed on 5/31/62 at Seven Pines, VA.

PAGE, J.
A resident of Wilson County, NC. Enlisted as a Private. Paroled on 5/6/65 at Greensboro, NC.

PARKER, Samuel Y.
21 years old, a resident of Wilson County, NC. Enlisted 6/28/61 at Craven County, NC as a Sergeant. Promoted 1st Sergeant on 11/30/61. Promoted 2nd Lieutenant on 6/10/62. Promoted 1st Lieutenant on 3/9/63. Killed on 5/3/63 at Chancellorsville, VA.

PATTON, Henry D.
33 years old, a resident of Wilson County, NC. Enlisted 6/28/61 at Craven County, NC as a Musician. Transferred to Confederate Navy on 10/2/63.

PENDER, Cadmus C.
18 years old, a resident of Wilson County, NC. Enlisted 6/28/61 at Craven County, NC as a Private. Died on 2/22/62 at Manassas, VA.

PITTMAN, Kinchen
22 years old, a resident of Wilson County, NC. Enlisted 6/28/61 at Craven County, NC as a Private. Captured on 5/19/65 at Spotsylvania Court House, VA. Died on 2/19/65.

PRIDGEN, Hugh F.
21 years old, a resident of Wilson County, NC. Enlisted 6/28/61 at Craven County, NC as a Private. Killed on 5/3/63 at Chancellorsville, VA.

RENTFROW, David
21 years old, a resident of Wilson County, NC. Enlisted 6/28/61 at Craven County, NC as a Private. Killed on 5/31/62 at Seven Pines, VA.

RHODES, Bennett B.
28 years old, a resident of Wilson County, NC. Enlisted 6/28/61 at Craven County, NC as a Private. Wounded on 12/13/62 at Fredricksburg, VA. Returned to regiment on 5/1/63. Absent without leave on 3/11/65.

ROBERSON, Andrew J.
34 years old, a resident of Wilson County, NC. Enlisted 6/28/61 at Craven County, NC as a Private. Killed on 5/3/63 at Chancellorsville, VA.

ROSS, David Y.
22 years old, a resident of Wilson County, NC. Enlisted 6/28/61 at Craven County, NC as a Private. Wounded on 12/14/62 at South Mountain, MD. Died of wounds on 12/16/62.

ROWE, Joseph W.
35 years old, a resident of Wilson County, NC. Enlisted 2/12/62 at Wilson County, NC as a Private. Killed on 9/14/62 at South Mountain, MD.

SASSER, Phillip E.
37 years old, a resident of Wilson County, NC. Enlisted 6/28/61 at Craven County, NC as a Private. Killed on 12/13/62 at Fredricksburg, VA.

SASSER, Sugars A.
26 years old, a resident of Wilson County, NC. Enlisted 6/28/61 at Craven County, NC as a Private. Surrendered on 4/9/65 at Appomattox Court House, VA.

SCOTT, Seth H.
20 years old, a resident of Wilson County, NC. Enlisted on 6/28/61 at Craven County, NC as a Private. Wounded on 5/31/62 at Seven Pines, VA. Hospitalized on 6/2/62 at Richmond, VA. Missing in action on 5/3/62 at Chancellorsville, VA.

SHARPE, Abraham M.
21 years old, a resident of Wilson County, NC. Enlisted on 6/28/61 at Craven County, NC as a Private. Wounded on 5/31/62 at Seven Pines, VA. Died of wounds at Wilson County, NC.

SIMMS, Patrick Henry
27 years old, a resident of Wilson County, NC. Enlisted on 5/16/61 at Wilson County, NC as a 2nd Lieutenant. Promoted 1st Lieutenant on 5/31/62. Wounded in action. Resigned on 2/7/63.

SMITH, Henry
Enlisted on 11/1/63 at Wake County, NC as a Private.

SNOW, James
39 years old, a resident of Alexander County, NC, occupation a farmer. Enlisted on 10/9/61 as a Private. Mustered on 11/20/61 into Co. G, 37 North Carolina Infantry. Wounded on 12/13/62 at Fredricksburg, VA. Transferred to Co. F, 4 North Carolina Infantry on 3/28/64.

SOMERS, M.
Enlisted as a Private. Paroled on 5/13/65 at Greensboro, NC.

STEVENS, William Virgil
20 years old, a resident of Wilson County, NC. Enlisted 6/28/61 at Craven County, NC as a Corporal. Promoted Sergeant. Promoted 2nd Lieutenant on 2/21/63. Killed at Chancellorsville, VA on 5/3/63.

STEWART, Zebulon M. P.
28 years old, a resident of Wilson County, NC. Enlisted 6/28/61 at Craven County, NC as a Private. Wounded on 5/31/62 at Seven Pines, VA. Detailed as Provost Guard from 2/5/64 through 12/15/64.

STITH, Thomas B.
18 years old, a resident of Wilson County, NC. Enlisted 6/28/61 at Craven County, NC as a Private. Promoted Corporal on 9/30/61. Promoted Sergeant on 1/22/63. Promoted 2nd Lieutenant on 8/2/63. Killed on 5/19/64 at Spotsylvania Court House, VA.

STOKES, Bryant
44 years old, a resident of Wilson County, NC. Enlisted 6/28/61 at Craven County, NC as a Private. Captured on 9/19/64 at Winchester, VA. Confined on 9/22/64 at Point Lookout, MD. Exchanged on 2/15/65 at Cox's Landing, James River, VA.

TAYLOR, Burrlee
20 years old, a resident of Wilson County, NC. Enlisted 6/28/61 at Craven County, NC as a Private. Died of disease on 1/15/62 at Manassas, VA.

TAYLOR, Joel
25 years old, a resident of Wilson County, NC. Enlisted 6/28/61 at Craven County, NC as a Private. Wounded on 5/31/62 at Seven Pines, VA. Returned to regiment on 5/1/63. Captured on 9/19/64 at Winchester, VA. Confined on 9/22/64 at Point Lookout, MD. Exchanged on 3/18/65 at Boulware's Wharf, VA.

THOMAS, Alfred
26 years old, a resident of Wilson County, NC. Enlisted 6/28/61 at Craven County, NC as a Private. Died of wounds on 6/28/62.

THOMPSON, Thomas E.
22 years old, a resident of Wilson County, NC. Enlisted 5/16/61 at Craven County, NC as a 2nd Lieutenant. Wounded on 12/13/62 at Fredricksburg, VA. Promoted Captain on 3/19/63. Wounded on 7/3/63 at Gettysburg, PA. Resigned on 9/20/64.

TODD, William T.
21 years old, a resident of Wilson County, NC. Enlisted 2/28/62 at Wilson County, NC as a Private. Killed on 5/31/62 at Seven Pines, VA.

VALENTINE, John F.
33 years old, a resident of Wilson County, NC. Enlisted 6/28/61 at Craven County, NC as a Private. Captured on 9/22/64 at Fisher's Hill, VA. Confined on 9/25/64 at Point Lookout, MD. Exchanged on 3/19/65 at Boulware's Wharf, VA.

VICK, David
21 years old, a resident of Wilson County, NC. Enlisted 1/20/62 at Staunton, VA as a Private. Wounded on 5/31/62 at Seven Pines, VA. Died of Typhoid Fever on 2/1/63 at Wilson County, NC.

VICK, Robert
18 years old, a resident of Wilson County, NC. Enlisted 3/12/62 at Staunton, VA as a Private. Wounded and captured on 5/3/63 at Chancellorsville, VA. Hospitalized in Washington, DC on 5/5/63. Exchanged on 6/30/63 at City Point, VA. Detailed for hospital duty from 10/30/63 through 8/15/64.

WARREN, Henry May
25 years old, a resident of Wilson County, NC. Enlisted 6/28/61 at Craven County, NC as a Private. Promoted Corporal on 11/30/61. Promoted Ordnance Sergeant on 3/8/63. Promoted 1st Lieutenant on 5/3/63. Wounded and hospitalized at Richmond, VA on 3/26/64. Promoted Captain on 8/30/64. Captured on 9/19/64 at Winchester, VA. Confined on 9/22/64 at Ft. Delaware, DE. Took Oath of Allegiance on 6/17/65 at Ft. Delaware, DE.

WATSON, Applewhite
18 years old, a resident of Wilson County, NC. Enlisted 6/28/61 at Craven County, NC as a Private. Promoted Musician. Surrendered at Appomattox Court House, VA on 4/9/65.

WATSON, Gaston
26 years old, a resident of Wilson County, NC. Enlisted on 2/13/62 at Wilson
County, NC as a Private. Wounded on 5/31/62 at Seven Pines, VA. Detailed
for hospital duty from 4/10/63 through 12/15/64.

WATSON, Jesse
24 years old, a resident of Wilson County, NC. Enlisted 6/28/61 at Craven
County, NC as a Private. Hospitalized on 7/15/62 at Richmond, VA. Died of
disease on 1/1/63.

WATSON, John H.
21 years old, a resident of Wilson County, NC. Enlisted on 10/9/61 at
Manassas, VA as a Private. Promoted Corporal on 9/6/63. Died of wounds on
7/19/64.

WELLS, Joel T.
19 years old, a resident of Wilson County, NC. Enlisted on 6/28/61 at Craven
County, NC as a Private. Transferred on 4/4/63 to Co. E, 19 North Carolina
Infantry.

WELLS, John D.
21 years old, a resident of Wilson County, NC. Enlisted on 6/28/61 at Craven
County, NC as a Private. Captured on 5/3/63 at Fredricksburg, VA. Exchanged
on 5/10/63 at City Point, VA. Promoted 2nd Lieutenant on 8/3/63. Surrendered at Appomatox Court House, VA on 4/9/65.

WHORTON, F. T.
Enlisted as a Private. Captured at Winchester, VA on 9/19/64. Confined at
Point Lookout, MD on 9/22/64.

WILKINSON, James W.
24 years old, a resident of Wilson County, NC. Enlisted on 6/28/61 at Craven
County, NC as a Private. Killed on 5/3/63 at Chancellorsville, VA.

WILLIAMS, Malichi M.
22 years old, a resident of Wilson County, NC. Enlisted on 6/28/61 at Craven
County, NC as a Private. Discharged on 4/3/62.

WILLIAMS, Thomas
20 years old, a resident of Wilson County, NC. Enlisted on 6/28/61 at Craven
County, NC as a Private. Died of disease on 1/19/62 at Richmond, VA.

WILLIFORD, Benjamin F.
18 years old, a resident of Wilson County, NC. Enlisted on 6/28/61 at Craven County, NC as a Private.

WINBORN, James M.
26 years old, a resident of Wilson County, NC. Enlisted on 1/6/62 at Wilson County, NC as a Private. Detailed as a teamster. Surrendered at Appomatox Court House on 4/9/65.

WINSTEAD, George W.
19 years old, a resident of Wilson County, NC. Enlisted on 8/2/63 at Wilson County, NC as a Private.

WINSTEAD, James G.
A resident of Nash County, NC. Enlisted on 7/17/63 at Wake County, NC as a Private. Wounded on 5/12/64 at Spotsylvania Court House, VA. Returned to regiment on 6/29/64. Captured on 4/7/65 at Sutherlandís Station, VA. Confined on 4/10/65 at Point Lookout, MD. Took Oath of Allegiance on 6/25/65 at Point Lookout, MD.

WINSTEAD, William E.
34 years old, a resident of Wilson County, NC, occupation a farmer. Enlisted on 6/28/61 at Craven County, NC as a Private. Promoted Corporal on 7/1/62. Promoted Sergeant on 3/14/63. Wounded on 5/3/63 at Chancellorsville, VA. Returned to regiment on 8/15/63. Promoted 1st Sergeant on 9/1/64. Captured on 9/19/64 at Winchester, VA. Confined on 9/22/64 at Point Lookout, MD. Exchanged on 3/15/65 at Aikenís Landing, VA.

WOODARD, John B.
28 years old, a resident of Wilson County, NC. Enlisted on 4/16/63 at Wake County, NC as a Private. Captured on 5/3/63 at Fredricksburg, VA. Exchanged on 5/13/63 at City Point, VA. Hospitalized on 6/30/63 at Richmond, VA. Returned to regiment on 9/1/63. Wounded on 5/12/64 at Spotsylvania Court House, VA. Surrendered on 4/9/65 at Appomattox Court House, VA.

WOODWARD, James B.
24 years old, a resident of Wilson County, NC, occupation a farmer. Enlisted on 6/28/61 at Craven County, NC as a Private. Wounded and captured on 5/3/63 at Fredricksburg, VA. Hospitalized on 5/5/63 at Washington, DC. Confined to Old Capitol Prison, Washington, DC. Paroled on 6/25/63. Captured on 10/19/64 at Strasburg, VA. Confined on 10/22/64 at Point Lookout, MD. Took Oath of Allegiance on 5/14/65 at Point Lookout, MD.

WOOTTEN, William P
18 years old, a resident of Wilson County, NC. Enlisted on 7/9/61 at Northampton County, NC as a Private. Promoted Corporal on 9/6/63. Promoted Sergeant. Captured on 9/19/64 at Winchester, VA. Confined on 9/22/64 at Point Lookout, MD. Exchanged on 11/15/64 at Venus Point, GA. Wounded in action three times. Surrendered on 4/9/65 at Appomatox Court House, VA.

Battle Flag of the 4th North Carolina

Craig and Baker

Footnotes

[1] Fort Macon is located near Beaufort Inlet and was wrested from the Federal garrison by Captain Josiah Soloman Pender of Tarrboro on May 11, 1861.

[2] Margaret Parker Battle (b. Jan. 19, 1811, d. Jan. 6, 1889) is the mother of the Battle brothers. She was the daughter of Weeks Parker and Sabra Irwin. She married Amos Johnston Battle in Edgecombe County on January 7, 1830.

[3] The Wilson Light Infantry Company, the Goldsboro Rifles, and two other Companies were ordered by Governor John W. Ellis to join Captain Pender's Company. This company would later become known as Company F, 4th North Carolina State Troops Regiment, CSA.

[4] Thomas Stith (b. 1842, d. May 19, 1864), was the son of Buckner and Lucinda Stith of Wilson. He was appointed 2nd lieutenant on August 2, 1863. Stith would be killed at Spotsylvania Court House.

[5] Bennett Blake Rhodes, son of John and Rebecca Rhodes, married Martha Louisa Battle (b. July 20, 1837, d. Jan. 21, 1921), sister of the Battle Brothers after the war. B.B. Rhodes was superintendent of the hotel in Wilson before and after the war.

[6] The Reverend Needham Bryan Cobb, D. D. of Wayne County, was a Missionary Baptist Church minister who was commissioned by the chaplain of the 14th North Carolina Regiment on May 31, 1861.

[7] Colonel Charles Courtenay Tew had been commandant at the Hillsboro Military Academy and was commander of Fort Macon before assuming command of the 2nd North Carolina State Troops Regiment, CSA on June 20 , 1861.

[8] Camp Hill is located near Garysburg, in Northhampton County.

[9] George Burgwyn Anderson (b. April 12, 1831, d. October 16, 1862) was elevated to brigadier general on June 9, 1862.

[10] Edward Dudley Hall was captain of Company A, 2nd North Carolina State Troops Regiment, CSA He was later promoted to colonel of the 46th North Carolina.

[11] Manassas Gap, about six miles east of Fort Royal, is the lowest pass in the Blue Ridge Mountains.

[12] David M. Carter, Moore County, captain of Company E, 4th North

Carolina State Troops, became lieutenant colonel on June 19, 1862.

[13] William T. Marsh of Beaufort County was captain of Company I, 4th North Carolina State Troops. He died of wounds on September 24, 1862.

[14] This was a term used by Southerners that meant they would have their portraits made. These war-period pictures may be seen in *The Battle Book* (Montgomery, Alabama, 1930) It was from this portion of the letter that we took the title for this book. We found it ironic that George would so eloquently predict his death and in many ways speak for all those boys who entered the war never to return as the young, vibrant men they once had been.

[15] Sergeant William P. Fitzgerald (b. 1837, d. May 19, 1863). He was from Cumberland County, Virginia and had been a carpenter in Wilson before the War.

[16] Henry May Warren was a clerk in Wilson before enlisting in Company F. He became a captain and survived the War.

[17] William Sharpe Barnes was the brother of Jesse Sharpe Barnes. William was promoted to adjutant on March 14, 1863 and he survived the war.

[18] The First Battle of Bull Run otherwise known as the First Battle of Manassas was fought on July 21, 1861.

[19] John P. Clark (b. 1839, d. May 5, 1862) was the son of Pomerory P. and Susan M. Clark of Wilson. He became a 1st lieutenant in Company G of the 5th North Carolina State Troops.

[20] This refers to Kate Johnston Battle who was born in 1842. She married Reverent Joseph Henry Foy, D.D. on March 19, 1860. Dr. Foy was a distinguished minister and educator in North Carolina.

[21] Dr. William Bernard Harrell married the Battle Brothers' sister Ann Judson Battle on March 13, 1851.

[22] Captain Jesse Sharpe Barnes was the son of Elias and Mahala Sharpe Barnes. He was killed at the Battle of Seven Pines.

[23] Thomas F. Christman of Wilson patented his "new and useful machine for Raising Marl and Dirt" on June 22, 1858. His son Daniel Peter Christman was a policeman in Wilson after being paroled at Appomattox Court House.

[24] Jefferson Finis Davis (1808-1889) was president of the Confederate States of America.

Craig and Baker

[25] Leesburg is now a thriving suburb of Washington, DC, in Loudoun County, Northern Virginia.

[26] Jack Robinson was killed at Chancellorsville, Virginia on May 3, 1863.

[27] Lafayette Barnes was the son of Major Edwin Barnes and Teresa Simms. He was 1st sergeant of Company F and died of Typhoid fever at Plains Station, Virginia.

[28] Whitford B. Bowden was honorably discharged from Company F on October 19, 1861.

[29] The Reverend Amos Johnston Battle (b. Jan 11, 1805, d. September 24, 1870) was the son of Joel Battle and wife Mary Palmer Johnston of Edgecombe County. While in his twenties he was among several ministers who founded Wake Forest College in Wake Forest in 1835. The college would later move to Winston Salem, North Carolina where it has become the world-renowned Wake Forest University. The young Rev. A. J. Battle along with W. H. Jordan raised $21,000 for the school by May 1838. During our research he was said to be a prominent and influential Baptist minister. Yet it seems he later broke with the Baptist church and transferred his services to the Disciples of Christ denomination on May 22, 1852. Can this be correct since he raised $100 for the Wake Forest College in 1853? In the book, called *Forget Me Nots of the Civil War: A Romance Containing Reminiscences and Original Letters of Two Confederate Soldiers,* the writer (daughter-in-law of A.J. Battle) talks of her father as being an abolitionist. This created some confusion as to whether the Rev. A.J. Battle became an abolitionist when he joined the Disciples of Christ. Mrs. Laura Battle does refer to her father as "an abolitionist." However it is unclear as to whether she was speaking of Rev. Battle or her own father? One cannot know for sure. We did find that many Disciples of Christ members and leaders from around the country had been in favor of the abolition of slavery. The church hotly debated the issue on the floor of the 1863 General Convention, at the height of the War. But the denomination never became a true symbol of abolitionist reform. Since the Battle's owned slaves it remains unclear what the Reverend's position was.

[30] The Bowden family lived in adjoining Nash County. In some Wake Forest Birthplace records indicate that at times Rev. Battle resided in Nash county.

[31] General Pierre G. T. Beauregard (b. May 28, 1818, d. Feb. 20, 1893) supervised the reduction of Fort Sumter.

[32] This was Kate Johnston Battle who married the Rev. Henry Foy, minister, educator, and religious author.

[33] Bacchus is the Roman god of wine.

[34] Minerva is the Roman goddess of wisdom and learning.

[35] Miss Mollie Speed was another teacher at St. Austin's Institute which at that time was under the direction of Rev. Charles Force Deems.

[36] Lieutenant Patrick Henry Simms (b. Sept. 23, 1833, d. Feb. 12, 1864) was the son of Theophilus Thomas Simms and wife Abigail Sarah Julia Holland. He was forced to resign his commission on Feb. 7, 1863 due to illness.

[37] Lieutenant William Virgil Stevens (b. 1841, d. May 3, 1863, also of Company F, was killed in battle at Chancelorsville.

[38] Rapidan Station was seven miles north/north-east of Orange County Court House.

[39] Gordonsville was eight miles south of Orange County Court House.

[40] Centerville was about twenty-five miles west, south-west of Washington and seven miles north of Manassas.

[41] The Clark Mountains are about twelve miles south west of Culpepper.

[42] Malachi M. Williams was a printer in Wilson before the war. He was discharged on April 3, 1862.

[43] John W. Dunham was promoted to captain in 1862 but later resigned in 1863 because of his wounds. The Wilson County Chapter of the United Daughters of the Confederacy honors his name today.

[44] Major General John Bankhead Magruder held the same rank after the war under the Emperor Maximilian of Mexico.

[45] General George Washington began the siege of Yorktown on September 28. Lord Charles Cornwallis surrendered on October 17, 1781.

[46] George was wounded in the Battle of Seven Pines on May 31, 1862. He died at hospital in Richmond on June 6, 1862, without having regained consciousness.

[47] Colonel Albert Farmer was the son of Joseph and Mary Barnes Farmer. He had seven kinsmen in Company F.

48 Thomas Jonathan Jackson became a major general on August 7, 1861. He died on May 10, 1863.

49 Roswell Sabine Ripley was promoted to brigadier general on August 15 1861. He was born on March 14, 1823, and died March 29, 1887. The First and Third North Carolina Regiments were under his command.

50 John W. Hines of New Hanover County served in Company D, 3rd North Carolina

51 Dr. Roscoe G. Barham was a native of Virginia who was a Wilson County doctor before the war. He was appointed as the assistant surgeon of the 28th North Carolina.

52 Dossey Battle (b. July 12, 1842, d. March 28, 1900) was the son of Benjamin Dossey Battle and Henrietta Sabra Hearne Parker Battle. He first served in 2nd Company D, 12th North Carolina.

53 Former Virginian Caleb Parker was a successful coach manufacturer during this time in Wilson, North Carolina.

54 The Battle of Seven Pines was a ferocious battle fought on May 31, 1862. It is here that George loses his life.

55 Walker Anderson served as the ordinance officer of the Brigade. He was killed at Spotsylvania Court House on May 12, 1864.

56 Leon Boardman Harrell (b.October 9, 1861, d. August 9, 1862) was the infant of Dr. William Bernard Harrell and Ann Judson Battle. Ann is the sister of the Battle Brothers.

57 This stop on the railroad was about two-thirds of the way from Richmond to Fredericksburg.

58 Edward Stanley Marsh was from Beaufort County. He was appointed first lieutenant of the Company I, 4th North Carolina

59 The Battle of Chantilly occurred on September 1, 1862, in Fairfax County, Virginia a few miles north of Centerville.

60 Company B and part of Company D, Second North Carolina were also mustered from Wilson County.

61 Bunker Hill was about ten miles north east of Winchester, near the Virginia-West Virginia line.

62 The Battle of South Mountain was fought on September 14, 1862.

63 Boonesboro is thirteen miles north west of Frederick, Maryland which is forty-five miles from Washington, DC.

[64] Daniel Harvey Hill was appointed major general on March 26, 1862.

[65] Lawrence Augustine Stith was the son of Buckner and Lucinda Stith. He was a doctor in Wilson before and after the war. He became the assistant surgeon of the 2nd North Carolina.

[66] Seaton Gales was the son of a famous newspaper family in Raleigh, North Carolina. He accidentally drowned near Peoria, Illinois, long after the war in 1891.

[67] William Patrick Wooten of Company F was a cabinetmaker in Wilson after the war. He was paroled at Appomattox on April 9, 1865.

[68] Paris is about eighteen miles southeast of Winchester, Virginia.

[69] Port Royal is about twenty miles southeast of Fredericksburg, Virginia.

[70] John L. Burton was promoted to corporal on May 7, 1862. He died in the Federal Hospital in Fredericksburg from wounds he received on May 15, 1864, at Old Wilderness Tavern.

[71] Dr. William Junious Bullock (b. May 15, 1834, d. October 2, 1923) son of Bennett Bullock and Martha Barnes. Dr. Bullock married Caroline Parker Battle on February 7, 1861. In 1862 he had become captain of Company A, 55th North Carolina. On November 20, 1863 he was replaced by Captain Benjamin F. Briggs and transferred to the Medical Service. During the imposition of Marshal Law by General McAllister Schofield at the end of the war, Dr. Bullock was appointed captain of the Police Department of Wilson. After the war he founded Belhaven (we're assuming the hospital there) in Beaufort County.

[72] John C. Gorman was born in Alabama in 1835, moved to Wilson and became a printer before he joined the army.

[73] John B. Grimes was from Pitt County and was captain and assistant quartermaster of the 4th North Carolina.

[74] Strasburg is a railroad junction ten miles from Front Royal, Virginia.

[75] Daniel Harvey Hill was appointed to major general on March 26, 1862. He survived the war and lived until 1889.

[76] Hanover Junction is about twelve miles to Richmond.

[77] Richard Stoddert Ewell was promoted to major general on January 24, 1862. He survived the war dying at the age of 56.

[78] Alexander Miller was in Company K, 2nd North Carolina. He was from Craven County where he returned after the war.

[79] Williamsport is on the Potomac River several miles from Hagerstown, Maryland.

[80] William Bennett Nolly (1843-July 1, 1863), son of William and Charlotte Proctor Nolly of Edgecombe County, was killed at the Battle of Gettysburg.

[81] Culpepper is about thirty-five miles of Fredericksburg, Virginia.

[82] James Gay was was paroled a Appomattox Court House on April 9, 1865.

[83] John G. Valentine of Company F, 4th North Carolina was an engineer in Wilson before the war.

[84] James Thomas "Tom" Atkinson was the son of Lovet Atkinson. He was killed at the Battle of Spotsylvania Court House.

[85] Morton's Ford over the Rapidan River was about ten miles west of Fredericksburg.

[86] Cullen Andrews Battle (b. June 1, 1829, d. April 8, 1905) was promoted to brigadier general in 1863. He was related to the Battle Brothers but he is not their brother Cullen who shared the same name.

[87] "Pussy" was the family nickname for their sister Kate.

[88] Rappahannock Station, now known as Remington, was where the railway between Manassas and Culpepper crossed the Rappahannock Station.

[89] William Rufus Cox was wounded but not killed as was rumored at the time. He died in 1919 at almost 90 years old.

[90] Redmond Condon was a wheelwright in Wilson before joining the war. He survived but did not return to Wilson to live.

[91] Germanna Ford on the Rapidan River was about fourteen miles southeast of Culpepper on the way to Fredericksburg.

[92] Langley Mixon was a private in Company F. He later transferred to the Confederate Navy toward the end of the war.

[93] Robert Vick was the son of Elisha and Talitha Page Vick of Wilson County. He became a nurse in the Wilson Confederate Hospital after being wounded and captured while serving in Company F.

[94] For those of you who are not Southern, middling is the side of hog meat after the ham and shoulder are cut off.

[95] Robert Daniel Johnston was promoted to brigadier general on September 1, 1863. He died in 1919.

[96] William A. Driver joined Company F on April 4, 1863.

[97] Cullen Andrews Battle (b. May 8, 1848, d. March 22, 1909) was the younger brother of the Battle Brothers.

[98] Zebulon Baird Vance was governor of North Carolina from 1862-1865 and again in 1877-1879.

[99] Junious Daniel was fatally wounded at the "Bloody Angle" on May 12, 1864.

[100] Ambrose Powell Hill became lieutenant general on May 24, 1863.

[101] Cadmus Marcellus Wilcox was a native of Wilson County and was promoted to major general in 1863.

[102] Robert Emmett Rodes (b. March 29, 1829, d. Sept. 19, 1864) was mortally wounded at the Battle of Winchester.

[103] Jubal Anderson Early (b. November 3, 1816, d. March 2, 1894) was promoted to major general on January 17, 1863.

[104] Sister Caroline Battle.

[105] Matt Whitaker Ransom (b. Oct. 8, 1826, d. Oct. 8, 1904) was promoted to brigadier general on June 13, 1863.

[106] Robert W. Hudgins of Lenoir County was reduced from sergeant after being absent without leave. He repeated the offense several times but was returned later to Company D and was captured at Petersburg on April 2, 1865.

[107] Robert Frederick Hoke was promoted to major general on April 20, 1864. He survived the war and died in 1912.

[108] Plymouth, North Carolina, was captured from the North on April 21, 1864.

[109] Charlestown, West Virginia, is about twenty miles north east of Winchester, Virginia.

[110] Bunyan Barnes of Company F was the son of Elias and Zilpha Barnes of Wilson County. He was captured and imprisoned at Point Lookout Military Prison. He survived the war.

[111] Edwin Hooks Barnes, son of Drewry and Patience Hooks Barnes was confined at Point Lookout under an assumed name. He survived the war and died in 1915.

[112] Bryant Stokes was a carpenter in Wilson before the war. By the time the war started he had eight children with his wife Elizabeth Wells. They had married in 1841. He survived the war. It's unknown how many children he fathered after the war.

[113] Joel Taylor was also imprisoned at Point Lookout. He survived the war.

[114] This passage refers to Major A.G. Brady, of the United States Army.

[115] Drewry's Bluff was eight miles south of Richmond.

[116] Colonel Charles S. Venable was from Prince Edwards County, Virginia.

[117] The Way Side Inn was in Raleigh, North Carolina. Walter passed through on his way back to the 4th in Virginia after having been released from Point Lookout the first time.

[118] Irishman John McBride, a sergeant in Company F, returned to Wilson where he continued to be a watchmaker. He was paroled at Appomattox.

[119] Richard Henry Battle was the son of Joel and Mary Palmer Johnston Battle. He was a lawyer in Raleigh.

[120] The boy "Church" has been referred to by some as one of the Battle's slaves. Whether this is referring to the Raleigh Battle's or the Wilson Battle's is unclear. However, if the Rev. Battle did own slaves in the midst of the war it might mean that he was not the abolitionist as previously thought.

[121] Vidette was sentry duty beyond the army outposts.

[122] He is referring to little brother Cullen.

[123] Hatcher's Run is a few miles south of Petersburg.

[124] Joseph Jones was from Wake County. He was promoted to captain of Company K, 14th North Carolina on April 27, 1862.

[125] George Winstead was from Nash County. He enlisted in Company F on August 2, 1863

[126] William Gaston Lewis was promoted to brigadier general on May 31, 1864. He was born in Rocky Mount and died in Goldsboro in 1901.

[127] William T. Faircloth of Wayne County was appointed captain of 2nd Company, 2nd North Carolina. He was the Chief Justice of North Carolina Supreme Court from 1895 to 1900.

[128] General William Tecumseh Sherman, USA was one of the primary architects of the fall of the Confederacy.

[129] Basil C. Manley became captain of Company A, 10th North Carolina on May 8, 1861. He was from Raleigh.

[130] Bernard B. Guion succeeded B. C. Manley as captain of Company A on March 1, 1865.

[131] James J. Powell retired to the Invalid Corps on March 29, 1865.

[132] James McKinnon, Jr. became 2nd lieutenant of Company A on January 24, 1865.

About the Contributors

Joel Craig has been interested in the War Between the States since the age of ten. Currently, he is president of The Ulster County Civil War Round Table; a member of Company A, 5th NY Duryee Zouaves; and a member of the Company of Military Historians.

Craig is the editor of *Dear Eagle, The Civil War Correspondence of Stephen H. Bogardus, Jr., to the* Poughkeepsie Daily Eagle.

Editor Sharlene Baker is the author of the novel *Finding Signs* (Knopf). She is a writer and creative writing instructor.

CPSIA information can be obtained
at www.ICGtesting.com
Printed in the USA
LVOW04s0323071116
511905LV00013B/272/P

9 780984 552900